Every Day is a Tough Day

Steve Damron

ISBN-13: 978-1-7264-1429-6

CONTENTS

1   Chapter 1: The Committed Life   5

2   Chapter 2: The Devotional Life   33

3   Chapter 3: The Faithful Life   57

4   Chapter 4: The Pure Life   85

5   Chapter 5: The Temperate Life   113

INTRODUCTION

I have read the Navy Seal motto many times. You may not know what it is, so I will share it with you: "The only easy day is yesterday." That is a fitting motto for the Christian walk. Somehow, we have this idea in our head that there is supposed to be unquenchable hilarity in one's life once they accept Christ and choose His path for their life. The Bible does indicate that there will be joy and peace, but those may be through the midst of a storm. The Bible nowhere indicates that the life here on earth will be without struggles, trials, and temptations. In fact, the Bible indicates that the life here on this earth will probably have some serious trials and tribulations. Consider some of the following verses:

"If the world hate you, ye know that it hated me before it hated you. If ye were of the world, the world would love his own: but because ye are not of the world, but I have chosen you out of the world, therefore the world hateth you. Remember the word that I said unto you, The servant is not greater than his lord. If they have persecuted me, they will also persecute you; if they have kept my saying, they will keep yours also" (John 15:18-20).

"My brethren, count it all joy when ye fall into divers temptations; knowing this, that the trying of your faith worketh patience" (James 1:2-3).

"Marvel not, my brethren, if the world hate you" (I John 3:13).

The key to the Christian life is turning the tough days into victorious days. The Bible tells us that "greater is He that is in us than he that is in the world." The Bible also tells us that we can be "more than conquerors." One of the ways that a young person learns this is to study and build endurance and stamina that can "endure hardness as a good soldier of Jesus Christ." A young person must learn to build walls of defense against the sinful desires that wage war against his soul. Charles Bridges has observed that the person without self control is easy prey to the invader: "He yields himself to the first assault of his ungoverned passions, offering no resistance. . . . Having no discipline over himself temptation becomes the occasion of sin, and hurries him on to fearful lengths that he had not contemplated. . . . Anger tends to murder. Unwatchfulness over lust plunges into an abyss of misery and despair."

The desire of this book is to be a help to parents and young people to show them a few areas of study that can shore up weak walls in one's life. There have been many times that a young person or a parent has asked me when it (referring to the trial) would be over so that life could be easier. Sometimes, I would have to shrug and say that life is not always easier. I know of some dear saints of God that every day endure hardships physically, emotionally, or financially. However, those saints of God are experiencing God's blessing and see His power through their life. Every day may be a tough day, but it does not have to be a day of defeat. Every day can be a victorious day!

Steve Damron

CHAPTER 1
THE COMMITTED LIFE

WE ARE ALL COMMITTED TO SOMETHING IN OUR LIVES. WHAT ARE YOU COMMITTED TO? -GODLINESS OR WORLDLINESS?

PROVERBS 16:3
Commit thy works unto the LORD,
and thy thoughts shall be established.

I love the Biblical word "commitment." It is something lacking today. As a Christian, my prayer is that your life will be totally committed to God. This small book was put together with the idea of stirring the believer towards analyzing one's life in the area of commitment. May it be a help to you.

COMMITMENT

In this day and age there is a word in the English language that seems to have lost its definition and meaning to most people. We know the word, we read the word, we understand the meaning of the word; however, we often fail to live this word. We place our hopes, desires, and expectations on this word. We have others believe in this word and they, too, place their hopes, desires, and expectations on us because we use this word. However, we often damage, hurt loved ones, and destroy lives because we fail to fulfill the definition of this word.

DEFINING COMMITMENT

What is this word? It is a word that means an agreement or pledge to do something in the future or to continue something until completion. This word indicates something pledged. It is a word that alludes to the state or an instance of being obligated to a cause, task, or purpose. This word is the English Anglo Saxon word—Commitment.

We prefer to think of commitment as something that doesn't require any sacrifice. No sacrifice really means no commitment, and in a world where there's always something bigger, brighter, and newer around the next corner, most people find it less and less beneficial to commit. To make things harder, we often perceive some things to be better to or for us than they actually might be, and so we are confused as to what to commit. Nowadays it's a big deal to make an honest commitment because we don't like being obligated. Commitment is at the very heart of what it is to be a real man or woman. Commitment is to agree or pledge to do something in the future or to continue something until completion, see something through, regardless of the cost—not halfway—but all the way through. Life is full of necessary and required commitments. It is virtually impossible to live life and not commit to something. Throughout this life we live, we commit to jobs, banks, creditors, relationships, marriages, dreams, our pastor, our church, and Jesus Christ.

I clipped this interesting item from a local newspaper: "A bus driver became annoyed with his job because he had to wait seven minutes after every run near an open field which 'litterbugs' had made it into an unofficial dump. He often thought that somebody should do something about that unsightly mess. One day he himself decided to get out and pick up some of the tin cans and other debris which was lying all around. This improved things so much that he soon was eager to complete his route and spend all his free moments in cleaning up the area. When spring came, he was so enthusiastic about this project that he decided to sow some flower seeds. By the end of the summer, many were riding to the end of the line just to see what the motorman had accomplished by doing what he and others had only talked about before." The article reminded me of the tremendous gap that often exists in many Christians between talking and true commitment! Some Christians will complain and gripe about sin in their lives or complain about a lack of service in the church, but it is the committed person who will take the next step to actually implement a plan to follow through.

BREAKING COMMITMENTS

All too often we fail to live up to our commitments. So what if we break a commitment? We've all done it, and sometimes we have even felt bad about it. We've all made wrong turns and bad decisions in making commitments. I mean, it looked and sounded good when we heard it. We truly thought that this was what we wanted at that time and place, and we felt that we could truly do what was required. However, when things got uncomfortable, or the way got hard, or things didn't go as we thought they would, we began to have second thoughts about what we had committed ourselves to doing, and thus began the breaching of our committed contract-our given word. At that time we began to search for reasons to justify why we should not be obligated to honor or hold to the commitment we made. As Christians, we at that time fail to follow the example of Jesus Christ, who was the best example of true commitment—a real man who gave up everything for love till the end. Christ was a man who committed His life from the beginning so that we would not be bound to eternal damnation. "But God commendeth his love toward us, in that, while we were yet sinners, Christ died for us" (Romans 5:8). What if Jesus would have reneged or breached on His word, on His commitment to mankind?

There are close to 100 million church members in America, and yet, why are we not making more of a moral and spiritual impact? Why is it, that on Sunday morning, hundreds of churches have empty pews? Why are so many churches having just a few attend services on Wednesday and Sunday nights? Now, God knows if you can't be at church for whatever the reason (and He knows the reason). If you could be there and you're not, He knows that too!

The Holy Bible is the inspired, inerrant Word of God, and yet, why is it that so few read it? If God is a prayer-answering God (and He is), and if He meant for us to ask, seek, and knock, then why is so little praying going on? If you and I believe there is a heaven and hell, why do we keep so quiet about the gospel? If we believe that there is none other name under heaven whereby we must be saved, then why are we not sharing the message of His saving grace? I'll tell you why, there's a lack of commitment!

As we begin to look at this idea of commitment, let's consider some Scriptures.

PSALM 37:1-5

Fret not thyself because of evildoers, neither be thou envious against the workers of iniquity. For they shall soon be cut down like the grass, and wither as the green herb. Trust in the LORD, and do good; so shalt thou dwell in the land, and verily thou shalt be fed. Delight thyself also in the LORD; and he shall give thee the desires of thine heart. Commit thy way unto the LORD; trust also in him; and he shall bring it to pass.

Many folks look at this passage and reverse some of the verbage in the context. Folks read verse 4 and tell God that they do not have the desires of their heart, but they forget to delight in the Lord. Delighting in the Lord is, in essence, a commitment of one's will to find in what God would have us to delight. For this reason, I can dogmatically say that the absence of the Word of God and prayer in one's life will result in a lack of spiritual commitment.

PROVERBS 3:5-6

Trust in the LORD with all thine heart; and lean not unto thine own understanding. In all thy ways acknowledge him, and he shall direct thy paths.

Are you noticing a pattern developing with the idea of commitment? Our commitment begins with a belief and trust in the Lord. In order to have a path that is leading in the right direction, we must be committed to the Lord with all of our hearts.

Matthew Henry in his commentary on these verses shows the link between verses one through four in this context. He divides this short passage into three categories. We need to learn to rely on God's precepts shown to us in verses one and two. We then need to learn to rely on God's promises in verses three and four. This is indicated by binding God's Word around our neck. This binding about the neck could refer to the Eastern custom of writing a special name or even a god on papyri and then putting it around the neck as protection. God is instructing us to place the Scriptures as the final promise of God's authority and protection in our life. Matthew Henry continues his thoughts with concluding that when we keep God's precepts and learn to rely on His promises, we then can trust in God's providential working in our lives. You notice again that our commitment to God and His Word will help us in establishing our way in this carnal world.

LUKE 16:10-13

He that is faithful in that which is least is faithful also in much: and he that is unjust in the least is unjust also in much. If therefore ye have not been faithful in the unrighteous mammon, who will commit to your trust the true riches? And if ye have not been faithful in that which is another man's, who shall give you that which is your own? No servant can serve two masters: for either he will hate the one, and love the other; or else he will hold to the one, and despise the other. Ye cannot serve God and mammon.

These are the words of Christ, and we are going to consider them because of the word "commit" which is located in verse 11. I wanted us to look at what that words mean and then try to draw some conclusions. Commit means to deposit, to lean upon, or to trust wholly. Christ wants to commit to us the greater things that are eternal, but He desires us to be faithful or committed to His cause. Christ then gives us some helps to strengthen our commitment. In verse 10, Christ indicates that there is no small task. Being faithful to the meaningless task will help us in our commitment to the bigger task. Start with the small areas of your life and strengthen your commitment. In dealing with many young people, I often find that they have grandiose plans for 10 or 15 years from now. However, they will not be faithful in their daily walk with the Lord, will not be faithful in the menial tasks in their home, and will not be faithful to the smaller responsibilities of ministry in their church. God expects us to be trustworthy in all areas. We then see that God is watching whom we serve. We all can quote verse 13, "No servant can serve two masters." Do we really believe that in our lives? Are we trying to please the Lord and the world at the same time? These thoughts from this passage should be meditated upon. The verses need to be committed to memory and rehearsed often.

ROMANS 12:1-2

I beseech you therefore, brethren, by the mercies of God, that ye present your bodies a living sacrifice, holy, acceptable unto God, which is your reasonable service. And be not conformed to this world: but be ye transformed by the renewing of your mind, that ye may prove what is that good, and acceptable, and perfect, will of God.

The last set of verses we are looking at to begin our thoughts with commitment deals with our surrender to our Savior. Notice that the verses give us a word picture of an altar. If we visualize the Old Testament saint coming to the tabernacle or the temple, he would be bearing sacrificial offerings that were a cost to him personally. Whether they were turtledoves, a wave offering of first-fruits, a ram or a sheep, there would have been some sweat and tears into the offerings. In this picture, God knows what He is asking us to commit to Him. Our lives are that which we consider most sacred. Most men and women do not purposely make it tough on themselves. We pamper and pay attention to ourselves way too much. So God wants us to commit to Him that which is most dear and allow Him to take our lives and transform them into amazing items of glory for the Lord. Verse 2 uses the word that has the idea of metamorphosis. The English word in the verse is "transformed". A caterpillar is changed from something that crawls in the dirt and is confined to a small little world view into a being that has wings and takes flight. The world is a different place. As we looked at a few Scriptures in relation to commitment, are you willing to place your trust in the Word of God and give your life fully into the hands of God?

Frances Havergal, the songwriter, lived and moved according to the Word of God. His Word was her constant companion. On the last day of her life, she asked a friend to read to her the forty-second chapter of Isaiah. When the friend read the sixth verse, "I the Lord have called thee in righteousness, and will hold thine hand, and will keep thee," Miss Havergal stopped her. She whispered, "Called-held-kept. I can go home on that!" And she did go home on that. She found His promises unfailing. She learned that committing her life to the Lord was worth living and dying for.

ARE YOU COMMITTED TO GOD?

As we consider being committed, let's first look at ways we should be committed to God. You have probably heard of a few excuses why people do not attend church. I listed a few together over the next paragraph.

I cannot attend church because ... Sunday is my only time at home. I am to have company. I would rather insult God than invite my company to go with me or to stay at home until I return from church. I am going to visit others. They are important to me, and I want them to know how much I think of them. I have some work to do around the house. I want to be with my family at home, for it is much better to be with my family at home than to be with God and His family at church. I don't like some of the people who attend my church. They are too much like me for anybody to like. I'm just out of the habit of going. I just don't feel like going. I've been going to too many other places. I am not really interested. I know Christ died for me and for His church, but actually I don't care if the church closes its doors. I think I'll just use God's day for myself. I'll read the paper, take a drive in the afternoon, and watch a show Sunday night. God will never know the difference, and I'll get the benefit of my money all to myself.

Friend, if you should use one or more of these excuses for missing the services of worship, please tear this out, sign your name, and lay it at the foot of the cross. Can you do that?

MARK 12:30

And thou shalt love the Lord thy God with all thy heart, and with all thy soul, and with all thy mind, and with all thy strength: this is the first commandment.

MATTHEW 6:33

But seek ye first the kingdom of God, and his righteousness; and all these things shall be added unto you.

My commitment to God must be all day, every day. We must understand that commitment to God does not have an on and off switch. Real commitment is not a Sunday thing, it's 24 hours a day, 7 days a week, 365 days a year, with no vacations or off days. You are the same person on Monday through Saturday as you are on Sunday. Recently, my wife was sharing the gospel with a lady in town. She and another member of our church took a lady out to lunch because the lady was interested in finding more out about the Lord. Through the course of conversation, this lady mentioned that she and her husband do not attend any churches at the present time because nobody seems to live Christ during the week. The world is looking for something different than just a Sunday go to meetin' religion. Is this your religion? Christ wants to come and transform your life. This occurs when He has free reign in all of the crevices of your heart.

My commitment to God must be visible. If we are really committed to God, it will show. Others will see the fruits of your commitment. They should see the same person on Monday through Saturday as they see on Sunday. Strength in my commitment is built when others see it displayed. I must be in practice as a Christian. I would challenge you to sit and read the book of James in one sitting. Do this a couple of times and ask God to show you some of the meaning that He desires you to receive from this book. No doubt, God will impress you to be a doer of the Word. You will see that your works, your tongue, your giving—jj all need to be committed to the Lord. Faith in action requires a heart that is committed to the Lord.

So, we have seen that commitment to God is daily rejuvenated, and my commitment must be visibly displayed.

Commitment isn't something you put on and take off like a suit.

ARE YOU COMMITTED TO FAMILY?

This is an item that is so lacking in our society. This lack of commitment starts from the top, the husband and father. We have barrenness in our nation of fathers that are committed to their families. No wonder that 50% of all marriages end in divorce, and, sadly, children see no commitment to family from their parents. Dads and moms need to be committed to being with their children and spending time with their children. Over the years, I have encountered some parents that seem to want to find any way to get away from their children. After spending some time with their children, I believe I understood why they desired this, but their behavior was reflecting their parents' lack of commitment to one of God's established institutions. Dad and mom should weekly be finding time to spend in rearing their children. The Bible says that children are a heritage from the Lord.

A cute little girl was sitting on top of a pile of luggage in a hotel lobby. Her parents were at the desk registering for their room. A sympathetic lady asked the little girl if they were visiting relatives in the city. "Oh, no," the girl replied, "we're going to live at this hotel until we find a house. My Daddy has a new job, and we had to sell our house and move." The lady said, "Oh, it's too bad you don't have a home." To which the girl replied, "Oh, we have a home—it's just that we don't have a house to put it in." I give this illustration to dads and moms because my home is the important item, not the house in which I am abiding. The externals seem to matter so much today, but the internal workings of the home are what really makes the home a Biblical dwelling.

However, young people should still obey God's command to honor and obey in the home.

DEUTERONOMY 5:16

Honour thy father and thy mother, as the LORD thy
God hath commanded thee; that thy days may be
prolonged, and that it may go well with thee.

God desires children and young people to follow God's guidelines. We live in an age of rebellion and anti-authority. As I have studied the concept of why I am a Baptist, a thought has occurred to me many times. Many people have joined the Baptist movement, not because they believe in all the principles of the Baptist, but because they heard that Baptists were independent. For many, independence means rebellion. They get to do whatever they want, and nobody gets to tell them what to do. This attitude has transferred right into the average home, and we love to claim independence as a teenager. Sadly, our young people have learned this from watching some of the average church members in the local church. Our independent spirit is tempered by our submission to God's Word and God's authority, the local church. Remember, Paul told Timothy that the local church was the pillar and ground of the truth.

As a youth in your home, Have you let your parents know how much they mean to you? Have you actually told them over the course of this past year? Be committed to your family as a young person.

ARE YOU COMMITTED TO GOD'S CHURCH?

Finally, let's consider your commitment to church. You should be committed to attending your local church. Does your family need to ask, "Are we going to church today?" Does the "Sundayitus" epidemic seem to strike your life when the word "church" is used? What are some signs?

One sneeze and back to bed you go; however, on Monday grab a hanky and go to work.

Sunday nights, you are just too tired because you have work on Monday; however, on Friday and Saturday, you can stay up until midnight or later for your own personal hobbies.

Midweek service is so tiring, and we do know that where two or three are gathered together …. me, myself, and I seem to be able to hold a prayer meeting around my Internet search engine. The Word of God in Hebrews 10 still commands us to not forsake the assembling of ourselves together. Church is a very important part of a believer's life and as a young person, start making it a priority.

You should also be committed to church growth. When you believe in something, you tell others about how good it is. How many people did you talk to this week? How many did you talk to about Christ? We should be actively trying to get folks to go to church. It is a vital part of a Christian's walk with the Lord. There are a lot of Christians who say that they love the Lord, but they don't love the things that God loves. In Ephesians 5, we are told that Christ shed His blood for the church.

Are you also committed to the needs of the Church? "Watch out," you say, "Don't use that horrible word, TITHING." We need to be committed to giving to the church. In fact, let's go a step further. Let's say that if anything needs to be done, let's plan on your doing it for the church. The story is told of four people: everybody, somebody, anybody, and nobody. There was an important job to do, and everybody thought that somebody would do it. Anybody could have done it, but none of them did it, so it didn't get done. Somebody got angry, because it was everybody's job. Everybody thought for sure that somebody would do it, but nobody asked anybody. In the end the job wasn't done, and everybody blamed somebody, when nobody asked anybody.

You might give the typical excuse in this area:

I can't talk to people—No problem; so you must never talk about anything else to anyone.

I don't know enough about the Bible—Whose fault is that?

My life is my witness—That is good, but that is not enough.

Put your other excuses down and you will find that it all boils down to COMMITMENT.

J. Oswald Sanders was nearing his 90th birthday when he died while working on his last book. Before he was 50 he was afflicted with arthritis so badly that he could hardly get out of bed. He could have taken a nice retirement. Instead, he entered the most procreative years of his life. At age 50 he left a prosperous career as an attorney in New Zealand to lead the China Inland Mission (now Overseas Missionary Fellowship). Remarkably, as he entered his second and third careers, he was totally freed from arthritis. After several years of leading the mission, he retired, only to take on the directorship of a Christian college. Another step downward. Then he retired again. A widower twice, he certainly deserved a rest. But rather than taking it easy, he accelerated, spending his last 20 years speaking around the world over 300 times per year. His respect grew even though he never sought the limelight or tried to maintain his position.

As we close with our thought, understand that you are committed to something:

Getting all the money you can;
Obtaining early retirement;
Keeping ahead of the Joneses;
Giving your children everything you didn't have;
Being uncommitted;
Getting all the pleasure you can out of life; or
Seeking the Kingdom of God and His righteousness.

Are you committed to right or wrong? Are you committed to truth or dishonesty? Are you committed to God or the devil? Are you committed to holiness or sinfulness? Your actions in this life tell others how you are committed.

Questions to Consider

1)

2)

3)

4)

ADDITIONAL HELPS
FOR THE LIFE OF COMMITMENT

THE CHURCH AND THE WORLD walked far apart
On the changing shores of time,

The World was singing a giddy song,
And the Church a hymn sublime.

"Come, give me your hand," said the merry World,
"And walk with me this way!"

But the good Church hid her snowy hands
And solemnly answered "Nay,

I will not give you my hand at all,
And I will not walk with you;

Your way is the way that leads to death;
Your words are all untrue."

"Nay, walk with me but a little space,"
Said the World with a kindly air;

"The road I walk is a pleasant road,
And the sun shines always there;

Your path is thorny and rough and rude,
But mine is broad and plain;

My way is paved with flowers and dews,
And yours with tears and pain;

The sky to me is always blue,
No want, no toil I know;

The sky above you is always dark,
Your lot is a lot of woe;

There's room enough for you and me
To travel side by side."

Half shyly the Church approached the World
And gave him her hand of snow;

And the old World grasped it and walked along,
Saying, in accents low,

"Your dress is too simple to please my taste;
I will give you pearls to wear,

Rich velvets and silks for your graceful form,
And diamonds to deck your hair."

The Church looked down at her plain white robes,
And then at the dazzling World,

And blushed as she saw his handsome lip

With a smile contemptuous curled.

"I will change my dress for a costlier one,"
Said the Church, with a smile of grace;

Then her pure white garments drifted away,
And the World gave, in their place,

Beautiful satins and shining silks,
Roses and gems and costly pearls;

While over her forehead her bright hair fell
Crisped in a thousand curls.

"Your house is too plain," said the proud old World,
"I'll build you one like mine;

With walls of marble and towers of gold,
And furniture ever so fine."

So he built her a costly and beautiful house;
Most splendid it was to behold;

Her sons and her beautiful daughters dwelt there
Gleaming in purple and gold;

Rich fairs and shows in the halls were held,
And the World and his children were there.

Laughter and music and feasts were heard
In the place that was meant for prayer.

There were cushioned seats for the. rich and the gay,
To sit in their pomp and pride;

But the poor who were clad in shabby array,
Sat meekly down outside.

"You give too much to the poor," said the World.
"Far more than you ought to do;

If they are in need of shelter and food,
Why need it trouble you?

Go, take your money and buy rich robes,
Buy horses and carriages fine;

Buy pearls and jewels and dainty food,
Buy the rarest and costliest wine;

My children, they dote on all these things,
And if you their love would win,

You must do as they do, and walk in the ways
That they are walking in."

So the poor were turned from her door in scorn,
And she heard not the orphan's cry;

But she drew her beautiful robes aside,
As the widows went weeping by.

Then the sons of the World and the Sons of the Church
Walked closely hand and heart,

And only the Master, who knoweth all,
Could tell the two apart.

Then the Church sat down at her ease, and said,
"I am rich and my goods increase;

I have need of nothing, or aught to do,
But to laugh, and dance, and feast."

The sly World heard, and he laughed in his sleeve,
And mockingly said, aside—

"The Church is fallen, the beautiful Church;
And her shame is her boast and her pride."

The angel drew near to the mercy seat,
And whispered in sighs her name;

Then the loud anthems of rapture were hushed,
And heads were covered with shame;

And a voice was heard at last by the Church
From Him who sat on the throne,

"I know thy works, and how thou hast said,
'I am rich,' and hast not known

That thou art naked, poor and blind,

And wretched before my face;

Therefore from my presence cast I thee out,
And blot thy name from its place."

THE CHURCH WALKING WITH THE WORLD
MATILDA C. EDWARDS

A Bible Study on Commitment

"When thou shalt vow a vow unto the LORD thy God, thou shalt not slack to pay it: for the LORD thy God will surely require it of thee; and it would be sin in thee. But if thou shalt forbear to vow, it shall be no sin in thee. That which is gone out of thy lips thou shalt keep and perform; even a freewill offering, according as thou hast vowed unto the LORD thy God, which thou hast promised with thy mouth" (Deuteronomy 23:21-23).

Consider what Matthew Henry says on the following passage:

> The performance of the vows wherewith we have bound our souls is here required; and it is a branch of the law of nature, Deuteronomy 23:21-23. (1.) We are here left at our liberty whether we will make vows or no: *If thou shalt forbear to vow* (some particular sacrifice and offering, more than was commanded by the law), *it shall be no sin to thee.* God had already signified his readiness to accept a free-will offering thus vowed, though it were but a little fine flour

(Leviticus 2:4, etc.), which was encouragement enough to those who were so inclined. But lest the priests, who had the largest share of those vows and voluntary offerings, should sponge upon the people, by pressing it upon them as their duty to make such vows, beyond their ability and inclination, they are here expressly told that it should not be reckoned a sin in them if they did not make any such vows, as it would be if they omitted any of the sacrifices that God had particularly required. For (as bishop Patrick well expresses it) God would have men to be easy in his service, and all their offerings to be free and cheerful. (2.) We are here laid under the highest obligations, when we have made a vow, to perform it, and to perform it speedily: "*Thou shalt not be slack to pay it,* lest if it be delayed beyond the first opportunity the zeal abate, the vow be forgotten, or something happen to disable thee for the performance of it. *That which has gone out of thy lips* as a solemn and deliberate vow must not be recalled, but *thou shalt keep and perform it,* punctually and fully." The rule of the gospel goes somewhat further than this. II Corinthians 9:7, *Every one, according as he purposeth in his heart,* though it have not gone out of his lips, *so let him give.* Here is a good reason why we should pay our vows, that if we do not *God will require it of us,* will surely and severely reckon with us, not only for lying, but for going about to mock him, who cannot be mocked.

Commitment will build a lasting trust and honesty in a young person. It is a quality which should be desired to implement.

Commitment is shown when one has an unwavering loyalty to responsibility no matter what the difficulty. A lack of commitment to Christ will cause great harm to an individual, in a home, in a church, or in a nation. Throughout history, we lift up those that were committed to a cause greater than themselves.

Examples:

Try to research each individual and put some pros or cons in regards to lessons on commitment.

Historical: George Washington

_____

_____

_____

Historical: Benedict Arnold (Negative Example)

_____

_____

_____

Biblical: Daniel and the three Hebrew Children

_____

_____

_____

Biblical: The Apostle Paul

_____

_____

_____

Questions to Ponder

Adapted from *Christian Character Studies*

by Gary Maldaner

Put a C for Committed to a good cause or a U for Uncommitted to a good cause next to the following phrases:

_____ A young man repeatedly allows himself to have sinful, immoral thoughts.

_____ A young man is involved weekly in ministry work such as Sunday School helps, visiting a nursing home, or knocking on doors in the community to share Christ.

_____ A man or lady continues to serve in their church even though their spouse dies of cancer.

____A soldier fights bravely for his country although it could eventually mean the loss of his life.

____ A young person speaks to his parents in order to undermine the authority in church or school.

____ A young person listens to music that his parents would disapprove of when they are not around.

____ A young person decides to ignore the gossip that is spread about another young person.

____ A young man does not read his Bible regularly, but does spend much time with the internet and video games.

____ A young lady while babysitting spends most of her night on the phone with friends.

____While the employer is not watching, the employee takes extra breaks that are not allowed.

Every Day is a Tough Day

Steve Damron

CHAPTER 2

THE DEVOTIONAL LIFE

VICTORY OR DEFEAT CAN ULTIMATELY BE TRACED TO THE EFFECTIVENESS OF A BELIEVER'S QUIET TIME.

GENESIS 5:24

And Enoch walked with God;
and he was not; for God took him.

What is meant by the term "quiet time"? This book is written to help explain the importance of the quiet time. Additional information is given to help believers see some practical helps in making their quiet time effective for strengthening their walk with the Lord.

DEVOTIONAL LIFE

When you create a memory, a pathway is created in your mind. It is like clearing a path through a dense forest. The first time you do it, you have to fight your way through the undergrowth. If you don't travel that path again soon, it will very quickly become overgrown and you may not even realize that you have been down that path. If, however, you travel along that path before it begins to grow over, you will find it easier than your first journey along that way. Successive journeys down that path mean that eventually your track will turn into a footpath, which will turn into a lane, which will turn into a road, which will turn into a motorway, and so on. The purpose for the illustration of developing a memory path is to show how important it is that a young person learns to have a quiet time as early as possible to develop a regular path to his time with God. This path then becomes a habit of life such as brushing teeth, cleaning hands, or bathing regularly. The pathway of a quiet time is one of the most vital habits parents, pastors, and youth pastors can help to develop in a young person.

The quiet time is one of the most important secrets of a Christian's daily life. There are countless examples in life to show that Christians who fail here soon grow cold and backslidden. It is of vital importance to learn what a quiet time is and how to adopt a regular routine.

Dr. E. Roste was the head of a mission training service overseas many years ago. He observed that they never knew which candidates arriving on the mission field would do well over the years, for it all depended on how well they guarded their quiet time. The Christian that perseveres in his quiet time grows steadily day by day with the Lord.

ABRAHAM AS AN EXAMPLE

"And Abraham gat up early in the morning to the place where he stood before the Lord" (Genesis 19:27). Abraham is an excellent example for maintaining morning quiet time. Notice the following things in regard to Abraham from this verse:

ABRAHAM GOT UP EARLY IN THE MORNING.

This is an excellent Christian practice. There are not many young people who cannot make this a practice in their life. Every once in a while, there may be a young person who is unable to accomplish this because of jobs that must be done very early in the day. However, a young person who has early responsibilities has times that they can spend time with the Lord during or after their scheduled responsibilities.

ABRAHAM HAD A SPECIAL PLACE TO MEET GOD.

It is important to establish a "go to" place where one can meet with God and have quiet communion with the Lord. This should be a quiet place, not one that is loud and disruptive.

ABRAHAM DID THIS DAILY, NOT SPASMODICALLY.

It is imperative that a young person develop a regular habit of a quiet time. Eating once a week is fine, but it would make a person very weak and sickly. So, in the spiritual realm, a young person who does not find a daily time with the Lord will struggle with sins that are common for youth. They will not experience the victory which comes by learning to lean on the Lord's strength. It is imperative to put helps in the hands of youth to establish them in the Word daily.

ABRAHAM STOOD BEFORE THE LORD, WAITING FOR THE LORD TO SPEAK TO HIM.

The quiet time is not for self-help thoughts or worldly meditative practices. The quiet time is to be before the Lord and to get close to our Creator and Savior. It is imperative that we learn to stand before the Lord and to obtain the direction and guidance that He would have for us daily.

II PETER 3:18

But grow in grace, and in the knowledge of our Lord and Savior Jesus Christ.

The plant requires air, sunshine, and food to grow; our physical bodies require food, sunshine, and exercise; and so our spirit requires nourishment every day of our Christian life. David says in

Psalm 5:3, "My voice shalt thou hear in the morning, O LORD; in the morning will I direct my prayer unto thee, and will look up."

Jesus not only prayed in the morning but He also sometimes prayed all night. "He . . . continued all night in prayer" (Luke 6:12). This is also seen in Matthew 14:2-3. Jesus' example and the experience of older Christians become a great motivation for observing a daily quiet time with the Lord and His precious Word.

WHEN I STOP AND PRAY

When the storm clouds boil around me,
And the lightning splits the sky—.
When the howling wind assails me,
And life's sea is rolling high—
When my heart is filled with terror,
And my fears, I can't allay—
Then I find sweet peace and comfort,
When I simply stop and pray.

When the things of life confound me,
And my faith is ebbing low—
When my trusted friends betray me,
And my heart is aching so—
When the night seems black and endless,
And I long for light of day—
Then I find a silver dawning,
When I simply stop and pray.

There are things beyond the heavens
I can't begin to understand,
But I know that God is living,
And I know He holds my hand.

Yes, I know He watches o'er me
All the night and all the day—
And He's always there to hear me
When I simply stop and pray.

Let's look at a couple of things to help a believer become more consistent in their daily walk with the Lord.

THE PURPOSE OF THE QUIET TIME

What is the purpose of having a quiet time? Many young people start questioning why things are done in their teen years. Many in authority get upset when this happens instead of directing their questions into a meaningful discussion of Biblical authority. The establishment of Biblical authority will cause the young people to become daily dependent on the principles of Scripture. It is important to establish their foundation on the Word of God as they learn to reason and make their own decisions.

FELLOWSHIP WITH THE SAVIOR

A consistent quiet time is so important to develop fellowship with our Savior. This is one of the basic purposes of the quiet time. God desires this communion even more than we do. The Father also desires our daily worship. There can be no relationship without a relationship. This may sound silly to put into writing. However, many folks say that they love the Lord and would never try to openly disobey the Lord, yet they do not work at developing a relationship with Him. They never know what God is leading them to do because they never talk to the Lord and go to His Word daily for leading in their life. It is important that we work at a relationship with the Lord. The two items for building an intimate relationship that have been given to us are prayer and Bible reading. If we neglect these two aspects, then we will never have the fellowship that God desires us to have with Him.

STRENGTH FOR THE DAY

A second purpose for the quiet time is to gain strength for the day. The Christian life is a battle against sin, the world, and the devil. Ephesians 6:12 says that "We wrestle . . . against spiritual wickedness in high places." It is vital that we gain strength to face these foes in our daily battles. The great example that is available to us is in the physical realm. There are those that can be extreme in their physical fitness habits, and most would testify that some regular physical activity prepares one for the rigors of daily life. A soldier that is going into battle goes through much physical testing and training. The soldier is preparing his body to endure the hardships of warfare. As Christians, we face warfare continually from the devil and his demons. It is important that we garner strength to counter the enemies' attacks. This can only be accomplished with a consistent, daily quiet time of Bible reading and prayer.

GROWTH FOR THE BELIEVER

The quiet time affords an opportunity for systematic Bible study and prayer. This will help the believer to grow spiritually over time. Maturation is not achieved overnight. Let's consider an agricultural example. What can a gardener expect in regard to a plant's maturity after planting seed in his garden? The gardener knows that the plant will only grow if there is consistent sunshine, watering, and weeding for the plant to mature. Notice that there is input into the plant in order for the plant to grow properly. The same is true for the believer. There will not be proper growth in a believer's life without the input of having a quiet time.

THE PREPARATION FOR THE QUIET TIME

It is always important to prepare for an upcoming project or event so that things will run smoothly. It is also important to prepare mentally for a test so that the stress of a test will not hinder one's memory of the facts retained in studying. In the same manner, it is invaluable to prepare so that a believer will gain the most out of a personal quiet time.

The story is told of early settlers in the Texas hill country. They came to a land lush with grasses and giant oaks. Their livelihood of animal grazing and farming, however, dried the rivers, denuded the soil of the grasses, and allowed cedars to proliferate. For years, the land died under the hard toil imposed on it. Then in 1928, when hill country farmers began clearing cedars from the land, they noticed a curious result. The ground in certain areas at first grew damp, then soggy, and finally gave birth to springs of water. For two generations, the cedars had gulped all the water and deprived the settlers of using the soil. After clearing away the trees, water ran so faithfully in some places that not even a nine-month drought diminished its flow.

BE FOCUSED

The Bible makes a promise to us—if we remove any hindrances to spending time in God's Word, it will pump endless streams of spiritual grace into our souls. It will become, as Jesus said, a spring of water welling up into everlasting life. This story reminds the believer to do what is necessary to prepare his heart for the reading of God's Word. When we diligently remove obstacles, the cleansing stream of the Word of God has the ability to flow into our hearts and renew us.

BE RESTED

Going to bed on time will immensely help the alertness and receptiveness of the mind to the teachings of the Word of God. Try as much as possible to avoid late nights and those activities that will disrupt a profitable time with the Lord in your quiet time. It is understandable that a schedule is not always locked in concrete, and there may come occasional interruptions that one would not expect. However, many times a believer allows interruptions that hinder a normal amount of sleep and cause wasted and unprofitable effort. These should be avoided so that the special time with the Lord remains intact. By protecting this quiet time with proper rest and fewer interruptions, a believer is placing a high priority on fellowship with the Lord. Maintain a stern discipline here, and God will bless you abundantly for it.

BE WIDE AWAKE

The next step is to make sure that you are wide awake before reading or praying. Many have found that washing their face with cold water or drinking a hot drink helps to make sure that they are awake. A believer needs to make an effort to be alert when they come to fellowship with the Lord. One man said, a cup of tea "helps me to have an intelligent quiet time." If you get sleepy on your knees, change your position. Abraham "stood." You can walk and pray out loud if that helps you to concentrate. Being alert is essential to getting from the Word of God what God desires for you. Take the necessary steps to wake up, and if you find yourself drifting off, then look at some change in your routine to help in this endeavor.

BE ORGANIZED

It is helpful to also have a clean area for reading and praying. Before reading the Scripture, put away distracting objects such as letters, mail, or pictures that may take your mind away from the Scripture and let it wander from the purpose at hand. In today's society, it can be common for folks to use a laptop or iPad for their Scripture reading. During the quiet time, make sure to turn off notifications so that you are focused on God's Word and not distracted by an update or a news alert. The believer should desire to have a time of solitude with the Lord that cannot be interrupted by phone calls, texts, updates, newspaper articles, etc.

BE LISTENING

As you approach your quiet time, it is not always necessary for the believer to do all the talking. Psalm 46:10 instructs the Christian to "Be still, and know that I am God." Stop talking and listen to God's voice. In Job 2:13, Job's friends sat down with Job for seven days and "none spake a word." This is something for believers to take note of. We have lost this wonderful art today of just being quiet. There is an old hymn that was written at the turn of the twentieth century. Its title "Blessed Quietness" tells us to seek for that quiet working of the Holy Spirit. The third verse says the following:

See, a fruitful field is growing,
Blessed fruit of righteousness;
And the streams of life are flowing
In the lonely wilderness.
Blessed quietness,
Holy quietness—
What assurance in my soul!
On the stormy sea, He speaks peace to me—
How the billows cease to roll!

BE YIELDED

The believer wants to yield to the leading, guidance, and blessing of the Holy Spirit in his quiet time. We are speaking of the preparation that should be made, and this working of the Holy Spirit is often forgotten in the daily life of a believer. The Holy Spirit should be evident in church services and in evangelistic outreach through soul winning, but the Holy Spirit should be evident in our daily walk with the Lord. Give the Holy Spirit a chance to work through your quiet time. Ask Him to be evident in enlightening the Scriptures and in leading your thoughts and prayers as you spend time alone with the Lord. One of the ways that the Spirit can have free reign in a believer's heart is to come before Him with a cleansed heart. "The sacrifices of God are a broken spirit: a broken and a contrite heart, O God, thou wilt not despise" (Psalm 51:17).

THE PROVISIONS FOR THE QUIET TIME

KING JAMES BIBLE

We don't have time to discuss all of the reasons why the King James Bible is the preserved Word of God. It is the book that God has blessed and is recognized by conservative scholars to be God's book for us in this age. There are many different types of King James Bibles. For instance, some Bibles have wide margins, some are hard bound or slim-line, others have devotional thoughts in them, and the list goes on and on. You may, over the course of years, find that there is one that you prefer. If you begin to dig into the Word of God, you will wear out your Bibles. This is good for a believer. C. H. Spurgeon said, "A Bible that's falling apart usually belongs to someone who isn't."

NOTEBOOK AND PEN

Have a notebook and pen to record something from the Bible. You may want a separate journal book to collect thoughts over time and then review them over the years. Some find that they like having a note study Bible with wide margins to put notes in as well as in the flyleaf of the Bible. There are many different ways to record notes or mark one's Bible. You may find that using highlighters or underlining certain Scriptures is what you like to do. In any of the cases, it is important that time is taken to think, meditate, and let God move in your heart through the Scriptures.

SEPARATE BOOK

Have a separate book with prayer requests and space to record the answers. Some churches use prayer handouts that are given weekly or monthly, and folks can use these to mark down prayer requests. It is very important to not just list prayers but to record answers. The Bible is filled with instructions to praise the Lord. Some of our prayer time should be in praising the Lord for answered prayers in our lives.

STUDY BOOKS

Some simple books that may help in studying Scripture are as following:
a.   Strong's Exhaustive Concordance
b.   Nave's Topical Bible
c.   Unger's Bible Dictionary
d.   Merrill's Bible Dictionary
e.   International Standard Bible Encyclopedia
f.   Wilmington's Guide to the Bible

THE PLAN FOR THE QUIET TIME

Try to prevent your quiet time from becoming mechanical. The Bible does say, "Where the Spirit of the Lord is, there is liberty." So, allow the Holy Spirit to guide you to verses that may be related to the subject you are reading. Allow the Holy Spirit to pause you in your reading and deal with your heart about a word or phrase that is in the reading.

Some other helps in planning your quiet time are to set aside the same time each day if possible. Also, aim at a systematic plan of reading and praying. Normally, you may spend half the time reading and half of the time praying. Don't be rigid in this plan or system. If the Spirit of prayer descends, continue praying. If the Word shines with new light, read on in the blessed Book and be filled with it.

A suggested order: a brief prayer, Bible reading, and then prayer. It is also helpful to have a way of proceeding through Scriptures. At first, when beginning a regiment of Bible reading, the idea of reading through the whole Bible may seem overwhelming. It is highly recommended to begin in the New Testament and set a pattern and habit, and then proceed to greater ventures of reading through the whole Bible. Reading the whole Bible should eventually be attained and made to be a goal either yearly or in more than a year. There are multiple Bible reading schedules which can be accessed from Bible websites that make it fairly easy to keep track of Bible reading.

Use the Word of God as a basis for praise and petition. This keeps the prayer from being the same every day. Learn to pray over the Scripture passage that you have just read. There could be a passage that speaks of specific attributes of God. Then, pause and think and praise God for that attribute. There could be a passage that directs your heart to some fault that may be in your life. Take the time to let the Scriptures transform your life. Pray through the Scriptures.

THE PRAYER OF THE QUIET TIME

Real prayer costs. It requires much time and discipline. Perseverance day by day is the real test. It will be a task that takes much diligence and steadfastness.

Have a journal or prayer sheet that you are regularly praying over and updating. A Christian should check the prayer list and notice prayer answers. Don't forget to thank the Lord for answered prayer. We often do not give the Lord His due glory and honor. The Bible tells us that God is a jealous God. One of the aspects that God is jealous of is the praise that is due to Him, "call upon me in the day of trouble: I will deliver thee, and thou shalt glorify me" (Psalm

50:15). Yes, call upon the Lord in times of need, but don't forget to glorify and praise the Lord.

Let your prayer be simple but very sincere. Just talk to God the Father as a child to his father. Many have used the following acronym to help with their direction of prayer. If this is a help to you, use it. (ACTS)

ADORATION—praise and worship of the soul to God. "O come, let us worship and bow down: let us kneel before the LORD our maker" (Psalm 95:6).

CONFESSION—repentance and turning from every known sin. "I acknowledge my sin unto thee, and mine iniquity have I not hid. I said, I will confess my transgressions unto the Lord; and thou forgavest the iniquity of my sin" (Psalm 32:5).

THANKSGIVING—thankful for anything, everything, joys, and sorrows. "Be careful for nothing; but in everything by prayer and supplication with thanksgiving let your requests be made known unto God" (Philippians 4:6).

SUPPLICATION—intercession, petitions, requests, and desires. "I exhort therefore, that, first of all, supplications, prayers, intercessions, and giving of thanks, be made for all men" (I Timothy 2:1).

Others have found that Christ's model prayer found in the Gospels is a good pattern for directing their prayers in an organized fashion. You can divide the Lord's prayer into five divisions and then pray through the different divisions with your own personal additions. The divisions are the following:

1. Praise— "Hallowed be Thy name"
2. Surrender— "Thy will be done"
3. Necessities— "Give us our daily bread"
4. Forgiveness— "Forgive us"
5. Adoration— "Thine is the kingdom"

THE PROBLEMS IN THE QUIET TIME

Satan will see to it that your quiet time is opposed every day. It will be a daily battle. If you miss a morning, it is not necessarily a failure. Confess the error and seek forgiveness the moment that the Holy Spirit reminds you of your inconsistency. Then get back into the habit. If you must stop at lunch to review some verses or some thoughts from the morning time of devotions, then by all means, take a moment or two to let the Lord use your quiet time to further impact your day.

Concentration will be a real problem. II Corinthians 5:10 indicates to us that we have a battle that is raging over our thoughts. The quiet time is a help in the battle of the mind. Remember that the devil does not want us to grow or to think on Christ or God. He will try to get our mind to wander. Work at this area and be sure that you are not giving the devil extra diversions to distract your mind during your quiet time. To get victory, you may want to meditate on the cross, the blood, and the mighty power of the resurrection. Those aspects of Christ's ministry of reconciliation have brought the devil to his knees.

I close with an illustration to encourage you to get at your devotional life and expect God to meet you there. As a drought continued for what seemed an eternity, a small community of farmers was in a quandary as to what to do. Rain was important to keep their crops healthy and sustain the way of life of the townspeople. As the problem became more acute, a local pastor called a prayer meeting to ask for rain. Many people arrived. The pastor greeted most of them as they filed in. As he walked to the front of the church to officially begin the meeting, he noticed most people were chatting across the aisles and socializing with friends. When he reached the front, his thoughts were on quieting the attendees and starting the meeting. His eyes scanned the crowd as he asked for quiet. He noticed an eleven-year-old girl sitting quietly in the front row. Her face was beaming with excitement. Next to her, poised and ready for use, was a bright red umbrella. The little girl's beauty and innocence made the pastor smile as he realized how much faith she possessed. No one else in the congregation had brought an umbrella. All came to pray for rain, but the little girl had come expecting God to answer.

REVIEW QUESTIONS

1. What is the major secret of a successful Christian life?
2. Give four good lessons that we can learn about the quiet time from Abraham.
3. Give three purposes of the quiet time.
4. List five hints to remember in preparation for the quiet time.
5. What lesson about the quiet time do we learn from Psalm 46:10?
6. Name three things to take with you in your quiet time.
7. Describe the division of time in your private quiet time.
8. How can one prevent the prayer from being the same each day?
9. What do you find to be the greatest hindrance to your quiet time?

ADDITIONAL HELPS FOR THE DEVOTIONAL LIFE

BIBLE VERSES FOR QUIET TIME

GENESIS 32:24-30

And Jacob was left alone; and there wrestled a man with him until the breaking of the day. And when he saw that he prevailed not against him, he touched the hollow of his thigh; and the hollow of Jacob's thigh was out of joint, as he wrestled with him. And he said, Let me go, for the day breaketh. And he said, I will not let thee go, except thou bless me. And he said unto him, What is thy name? And he said, Jacob. And he said, Thy name shall be called no more Jacob, but Israel: for as a prince hast thou power with God and with men, and hast prevailed. And Jacob asked him, and said, Tell me, I pray thee, thy name. And he said, Wherefore is it that thou dost ask after my name? And he blessed him there. And Jacob called the name of the place Peniel: for I have seen God face to face, and my life is preserved.

PSALM 42:1-2

As the hart panteth after the water brooks, so panteth my soul after thee, O God. My soul thirsteth for God, for the living God: when shall I come and appear before God?

PSALM 63:1-6

O God, thou art my God; early will I seek thee: my soul thirsteth for thee, my flesh longeth for thee in a dry and thirsty land, where no water is; To see thy power and thy glory, so as I have seen thee in the sanctuary. Because thy lovingkindness is better than life, my lips shall praise thee. Thus will I bless thee while I live: I will lift up my hands in thy name. My soul shall be satisfied as with marrow and fatness; and my mouth shall praise thee with joyful lips: When I remember thee upon my bed, and meditate on thee in the night watches.

GALATIANS 6:7-9

Be not deceived; God is not mocked: for whatsoever a man soweth, that shall he also reap. For he that soweth to his flesh shall of the flesh reap corruption; but he that soweth to the Spirit shall of the Spirit reap life everlasting. And let us not be weary in well doing: for in due season we shall reap, if we faint not.

II PETER 1:5-8

And beside this, giving all diligence, add to your faith virtue; and to virtue knowledge; And to knowledge temperance; and to temperance patience; and to patience godliness; And to godliness brotherly kindness; and to brotherly kindness charity. For if these things be in you, and abound, they make you that ye shall neither be barren nor unfruitful in the knowledge of our Lord Jesus Christ.

I JOHN 1:3-7

That which we have seen and heard declare we unto you, that ye also may have fellowship with us: and truly our fellowship is with the Father, and with his Son Jesus Christ. And these things write we unto you, that your joy may be full. This then is the message which we have heard of him, and declare unto you, that God is light, and in him is no darkness at all. If we say that we have fellowship with him, and walk in darkness, we lie, and do not the truth: But if we walk in the light, as he is in the light, we have fellowship one with another, and the blood of Jesus Christ his Son cleanseth us from all sin.

REVELATION 3:20

Behold, I stand at the door, and knock: if any man hear my voice, and open the door, I will come in to him, and will sup with him, and he with me.

THE ANVIL—GOD'S WORD

Last Eve I passed beside a blacksmith's door,

And heard the anvil ring the vesper chime;

Then, looking in, I saw upon the floor

Old hammers, worn with beating years of time.

"How many anvils have you had," said I,

"To wear and batter all these hammers so?"

53

"Just one," said he, and then, with twinkling eye,

"The anvil wears the hammers out, you know."

And so, thought I, the anvil of God's Word,

For ages skeptic blows have beat upon;

Yet, though the noise of falling blows was heard,

The anvil is unharmed—the hammers gone.

----UNKNOWN

Every Day is a Tough Day

Steve Damron

CHAPTER 3
THE FAITHFUL LIFE

WE CAN'T ALL BE PREACHERS, MISSIONARIES, OR SUPERSTARS IN THE CHRISTIAN LIFE, BUT WE CAN ALL BE FAITHFUL.

PROVERBS 20:6
Most men will proclaim everyone his own goodness:
but a faithful man who can find?

There is sometimes much "hoopla" made over someone who has achieved notoriety for a one-time bestseller or a one-time monetary success story. These, however, fade into oblivion and the man that is faithful in his daily walk with the Lord, faithful to his marriage and faithful to his church, is a rarity. Consider the word of the Lord in this area and may it challenge you to become more faithful.

FAITHFULNESS

When you think of the concept of faithfulness, what comes to your mind? I have had the opportunity a few times to visit Yellowstone National Park where the geyser, Old Faithful, is located. If you look into how the geyser got its name, you will see it is because of the exactness of its eruptions. It was faithful in regard to its consistency in actions. This is one of the characteristics of faithfulness.

DEFINING FAITHFULNESS

Consider one of the definitions of faithfulness: exact in attendance to commands. What does this mean? Exact means to duplicate or to adhere to specific guidelines that are given. Attending means to regard with observation and correspondent practice. So, the definition is pretty clear—to be a faithful or trustworthy young person is to adhere specifically to guidelines with observation and with actions.

I LIKE THE MAN WHO FACES WHAT HE MUST
WITH STEP TRIUMPHANT AND A HEART OF CHEER;
WHO FIGHTS THE DAILY BATTLE WITHOUT FEAR;
SEES HIS HOPES FAIL, YET KEEPS UNFALTERING TRUST
THAT GOD IS GOD; THAT SOMEHOW, TRUE AND JUST,
HIS PLANS WORK OUT FOR MORTALS. NOT A TEAR
IS SHED WHEN FORTUNE, WHICH THE WORLD HOLDS DEAR;
FALLS FROM HIS GRASP. HE DOES HIS BEST,
NOR EVER MURMURS AT HIS HUMBLER LOT,
BUT WITH A SMILE AND WORDS OF HOPE GIVES ZEST
TO EVERY TOILER. HE ALONE IS GREAT
WHO BY A LIFE HEROIC CONQUERS FATE.

Christ is our example of faithfulness. He was unwilling to give up; He refused to quit! The successful life prescribed by Christ requires faithfulness until death—a hand on the plow with no looking back, steadfast perseverance, racing hard for the tape, and fighting the good fight of faith. The devil loves it when we simply relax our efforts. He has a good day if we become discouraged. There are temptations to overcome, disappointments to handle, personal sins that beset us, burdens that depress us, and Satan is standing by urging that we quit trying. But wait—Christ is present (Heb. 12:3). Someone once asked James J. Corbett, at that time heavyweight champion of the world, "What is the most important thing a man must do to become a champion?" He replied, "Fight one more round." The Duke of Wellington said that the British soldiers at the Battle of Waterloo were not any braver than Napoleon's soldiers—but they were brave for five minutes longer. That is also true for the Christian in his walk here on this earth. A secret for success is: "Fight just one more round. Be brave for five more minutes." It is the difference between defeat and victory.

A BIBLICAL EXAMPLE OF FAITHFULNESS

In this study, we will look at a man who followed the definition of faithfulness pretty closely. As we consider these characteristics, look internally at your own life and ask God if you are trustworthy as His servant. Let's read from the passage of Scripture that contains the story of Abraham's servant.

GENESIS 24:1-4

And Abraham was old, and well stricken in age: and the LORD had blessed Abraham in all things. And Abraham said unto his eldest servant of his house, that ruled over all that he had, Put, I pray thee, thy hand under my thigh: And I will make thee swear by the LORD, the God of heaven, and the God of the earth, that thou shalt not take a wife unto my son of the daughters of the Canaanites, among whom I dwell: But thou shalt go unto my country, and to my kindred, and take a wife unto my son Isaac.

ABRAHAM TRUSTED HIM WHOLLY

The steward was not just fulfilling a task. He took interest in what his master had for him. His job was more to him than a paycheck.

You will notice that Abraham trusted him but wanted his word before he even began the operation. I believe that our Savior asks no less of us as His servants. He desires that we are committed all the way to Him. For in a duty which is to be performed for our Master, self-interest can often supersede the Master's bidding. We must swear our allegiance to our Savior and His cause. We can then proceed with our task.

The job that the servant was asked to perform is interesting. In teaching this passage to young folks, I often humorously ask them if they have an older friend that they would entrust with the task of finding a mate for life. This was no small task that the servant was asked to perform. The trust is enormous. Similarly, we as servants of the Savior are given an enormous task—to give the blessed gospel to the lost. This is our duty and task. Why would God entrust frail, fleshly men with the daunting task of helping with eternal destinies? This seems overwhelming, but the Master trusts his servants wholly with this task. How are you measuring up with the Savior's trust?

What does your boss think of you? To me one of the biggest embarrassments would be to have as my reputation that I just do the bare minimum. I want my reputation to be that nobody else has done as good a job. We are not doing this for our own pride, ambition, or reward. This is a serious calling from on high. This is the right type of reputation to have. Do you have that type of trustworthiness?

GENESIS 24:11-14

And he made his camels to kneel down without the city by a well of water at the time of the evening, even the time that women go out to draw water. And he said, O LORD God of my master Abraham, I pray thee, send me good speed this day, and show kindness unto my master Abraham. Behold, I stand here by the well of water; and the daughters of the men of the city come out to draw water: And let it come to pass, that the damsel to whom I shall say, Let down thy pitcher, I pray thee, that I may drink; and she shall say, Drink, and I will give thy camels

drink also: let the same be she that thou hast appointed
for thy servant Isaac; and thereby shall I know that thou
hast showed kindness unto my master.

THE SERVANT TOOK HIS JOB SERIOUSLY

It is reported that Michelangelo, while painting the matchless
frescoes on the high ceiling of the Sistine Chapel, spent countless
hours on his back on high scaffolding, carefully perfecting the details
of each figure. A friend once asked him why he took such pains with
figures which could be seen only at a distance by viewers. "After all,"
said the friend, "who will know whether it is perfect or not?" "I will,"
replied the artist.

As we read of artists or sculptors who are gifted, they seem to
care so much about detail which others don't seem to see. As a
Christian, there is a Biblical concept of doing all that we do to the
glory of God. The Bible gives us that instruction in the book of
Ecclesiastes and in Colossians.

ECCLESIASTES 9:10

Whatsoever thy hand findeth to do, do it with thy might;
for there is no work, nor device, nor knowledge,
nor wisdom, in the grave, whither thou goest .

COLOSSIANS 3:23

And whatsoever ye do, do it heartily, as to the Lord, and not unto
men.

Both of these verses instruct us to have a passion or intensity in
the endeavors that we undertake. So many people seem to care little
about the work that they are doing. Biblically, if we truly believe that

God has given us this task, then He wants us to put our hearts into the effort of the job.

As a young person, how much do you care about the tasks for which you are asked to do by your parents, by your teachers, by authority in your life, or by God Himself? He gives you jobs to do. Are you faithful to these jobs, or do you think of them as not important? I was talking with my wife about this recently. This is a weakness and a strength for me! Everything I am doing is the most important thing in the world for me to the extent that I tend to underestimate the importance of what someone else is doing. That is not the right perspective. I am not saying that you are the most important person in the universe. However, what God has for you to do is very important to you and God. Each of us is individually made and created by God, and our jobs are then specifically given to us by God. My job is not superior to someone else's job, but God expects me to take my job seriously.

Let me give you a couple of helps in this area of taking your job seriously. First, when you get up in the morning, you should remind yourself of God's top priorities for your day. As a teenager, it could be as simple as obeying with a right spirit or as complex as finding your vocation or future mate. When you see that God has a task for you every day, it brings value to your day. You will then redeem the time as Paul instructs in Ephesians, and you will not find yourself wasting energy or time on silly, trivial items. Pettiness can set into our lives and waste valuable time on items that have no lasting value.

Second, let God help you with your tasks. As a teenager, there are many who may discount your relevance to society, church life, or even home life. This does not discount your job in God's eyes. Did you notice that this servant realized his boss had a very important job, and he prayed to God? Include God in your daily routine. There are many tasks for you as a teenager to do, and God is concerned with the decisions that you are going to make. This is the beauty of developing a personal relationship with the Lord. You will find that God is concerned with the mundane details of your life, and He desires to lead and guide you through all that you do.

GENESIS 24:10

And the servant took ten camels of the camels of his master, and departed; for all the goods of his master were in his hand: and he arose, and went to Mesopotamia, unto the city of Nahor.

THE SERVANT TOOK ACTION IMMEDIATELY

We should be people of action. God has left us on this earth to accomplish His will, and we should be active in finding this will and doing it. I understand patience and waiting upon the Lord, but many folks seem to use that as an excuse to do nothing for the cause of the Lord. However, these same people seem to have a lot of activity in their lives for self-gratification and self-promotion. The only action that takes place for many people, as far as faithfulness, is sitting in a pew. This should not be. When you read the stories of men and women in the Bible, you will notice action. You see Noah building an ark for decades with his family and preaching to the lost. You see Elijah and Elisha active in dealing with kings, foreign armies, and everyday people in the land of Israel. You see David in the fields busy with his father's flocks, busy helping King Saul in his palace, and busy preparing supplies for God's temple. When you see David resting, he sins. Again, I am not saying that we should never pray, read our Bibles, and wait on the Lord. I am saying that we should be active in those areas which take work and then get active in the calling that God has for our lives.

The story is told of a young woman who was dressed as a rag doll. Melody Schick, 24, sat with a teddy bear cradled in her left arm and staring into space from a revolving platform. Only her eyes moved. Then, 5 hours and 43 boring minutes later she rose slowly and tried to smile. Miss Schick was seeking to beat the world record for sitting still! The previous record was 5 hours and 32 minutes. The record attempt took place at a Dallas shopping center as hundreds of shoppers watched. There are surely some saints in the church who could compete for that record. They have been sitting still—metaphorically if not literally—for years. They never become involved in the work of the local church. They criticize the church frequently, but they never participate in the program. This should not be true for a young person who is trying to establish trustworthiness in his or her life. You may not be the pastor, Sunday school teacher, bus captain, or nursing home leader. However, you can be saved, surrendered, and serving in the capacity that God has for you now. It may not be in the limelight, but it might be as a helper in the nursery; a helper taking the count on a bus route; or a helper at your church's VBS. As a young person there is much work that can be done in your own personal walk with the Lord, in your studies in school, and in your service at church. Are you taking action immediately to do what God has asked you to do?

GENESIS 24:54-58

And they did eat and drink, he and the men that were with him, and tarried all night; and they rose up in the morning, and he said, Send me away unto my master. And her brother and her mother said, Let the damsel abide with us a few days, at the least ten; after that she shall go. And he said unto them, Hinder me not, seeing the LORD hath prospered my way; send me away that I may go to my master. And they said, We will call the damsel, and inquire at her mouth. And they called Rebekah, and said unto her, Wilt thou go with this man? And she said, I will go.

THE SERVANT FINISHED HIS JOB COMPLETELY

He let nothing deter him from finishing his task that was set before him. How many little things get in the way of us finishing a job completely? We all can find excuses why we do not follow God completely when He gives us a command to do something. Your parents may give excuses why you, as a teenager, fail in certain areas, but when you face the Lord someday, your "mommy" will not be present to give the excuse to the Lord. As a young person, you need to get in the habit of finishing a job completely. I can remember having to learn this when I first started in the ministry. I was so consumed with the bigness of a youth activity and the fun of the activity that afterwards, I would sometimes forget the importance of cleaning the gym, the dining room, or the grounds where the activity took place. A day or two later someone would come and see me about an item left out or an area of our facility left looking shabby. It was a good lesson for me to learn that the clean-up from the event was just as important as the event. God is concerned about detail.

A challenge for you as a young person is to look at the detailed instructions that God gave in the book of Exodus for the construction of the tabernacle. It sometimes seems mundane and overly detailed, but God is concerned about the details. This is helpful for all of us when God gives us a task. We often get toward the end and want to short-cut the final step or two. Remember that our heavenly Father is concerned with our entire task. He wants us to get in the habit of finishing a job completely. I am glad that Christ has set this example for us. Christ came to this earth, and He accomplished some amazing feats. He was able to heal the sick, raise the dead, feed the multitudes, and stop the raging seas. However, that was not the ultimate task that God had for Christ. His task was to come and provide a way of salvation for all of us. Christ went all the way to the cross and could say with confidence, "It is finished." He came and completed the tasks that God gave him. This is why in Philippians we are told that Christ was obedient even unto death. His obedience is a testimony to you and me to complete the tasks that God has set before us no matter the hardness.

WHAT IS FAITHFULNESS?

A shepherd once came to the city of Edinburgh from the country. He had his small obedient dog with him. While there, the man died and was buried. That little dog lay upon its master's grave—not for a day, a week, or a month, but for 12 years. Every day at one o'clock a gun was fired in the castle of Edinburgh. When the gun was fired the dog would run to the local baker who gave it food and water. Then back to the grave it would go. This continued till the dog died 12 years later. That was faithfulness!

George Mueller prayed for 52 years for a certain man to come to Christ. A pastor visited an elderly man 21 times before being admitted, but then he befriended the man and led him to Christ. That was faithfulness! A Welsh postman had the British Empire Medal conferred upon him by Queen Elizabeth because he had not missed a day's service in 43 years. Paul Dhrlick, the chemist, performed 605 unsuccessful experiments—the 606th was a success! Thomas Edison made 18,000 experiments before he perfected the arc light. After experiencing 50 failures on another project he said, "I have found 50 ways it cannot be done!" That was faithfulness!

Are you not glad that Jesus was faithful in dying for us and that He now lives and is faithful to care for us? God grant us grace to be faithful!

REVIEW QUESTIONS

1. Define faithfulness in the 1828 Webster's dictionary.
2. What is one of the important tasks that has been given to Christians? Why must we do this task?
3. What are two characteristics that should be evident in a Christian's life when doing the Lord's work?
4. Where should my priorities be allocated? Are there multiple people that a young person answers to?
5. What are two ways that you can be faithful in society, in church and in your home?
6. If you are never called to lead a church or large organization, we should still be faithful. List three areas that every Christian can be faithful in.
7. Is God concerned about detail? List some examples to reveal this.

APPENDIX SECTION:

I am including some worksheets to help in evaluating some of your trustworthiness. These sheets will reveal weaknesses and strengths in your life. I would recommend taking your time through the evaluation process and get some authority to help you. The first sheet is for evaluating your ministry work in your local church. Get the leader to help tutor you in bettering your work in the ministry you are involved with. After a few training times, have the ministry leader evaluate your work and then endeavor to improve.

EVALUATE YOUR SERVICE

Ministry Evaluation Sheet

Teacher: Class:

Worker: Date:

Story / Preaching

_____

_____

_____

Games

_____

_____

_____

Songs

_____

_____

_____

Verse

_____

_____

_____

Additional Comments

_____

_____

_____

EVALUATE YOUR TIME

This next sheet is a simple time log to help you see if you are trustworthy with the time God has given you. This should be done with someone else verifying what you are putting into the log. We have a tendency to overexaggerate our business and time. By having someone verify, you will have the most accurate account of your weekly time.

Time Management Worksheet

Week _____

Time	Sunday	Monday	Tuesday	Wednes day	Thursday	Frid ay	Satur day
7:00 a.m.							
8:00 a.m.							
9:00 a.m.							
10:00 a.m.							
11:00 a.m.							
12:00 p.m.							
1:00 p.m.							
2:00 p.m.							
3:00 p.m.							
4:00 p.m.							

	Sunday	Monday	Tuesday	Wednesday	Thursday	Friday	Saturday
5:00 p.m.							
6:00 p.m.							
7:00 p.m.							
8:00 p.m.							
9:00 p.m.							

Time Management Worksheet

Week _____

Time	Sunday	Monday	Tuesday	Wednesday	Thursday	Friday	Saturday
7:00 a.m.							
8:00 a.m.							
9:00 a.m.							

10:00 a.m.							
11:00 a.m.							
12:00 p.m.							
1:00 p.m.							
2:00 p.m.							
3:00 p.m.							
4:00 p.m.							
5:00 p.m.							
6:00 p.m.							
7:00 p.m.							

8:00 p.m.						
9:00 p.m.						

EVALUATE YOUR SPIRITUAL GROWTH

Spiritual Growth Assessment

As you complete the assessment, avoid rushing. Listen for God's voice to encourage and challenge you. Consider this experience as one-on-one time with Him. Be intentional in your growth towards Christlikeness. Use the scale below to respond to each statement.

Never - 1   Seldom - 2   Occasionally - 3
          Frequent - 4   Always - 5

SPIRITUAL DISCIPLINES...

ABIDE IN CHRIST

I practice a regular quiet time and look forward to that time with Christ.____

When making choices, I seek Christ's guidance first.____

My relationship with Christ is motivated more by love than duty or fear._____

I get direction from the Holy Spirit in my devotional life._____

When God makes me aware of His specific will in an area of my life, I follow His leading._____

I believe Christ provides the only way for a relationship with God._____

My actions are directed to bring others to Christ._____

Peace, contentment, and joy characterize my life rather than worry and anxiety._____

I trust Christ to help me through any problem or crisis I face._____

I remain confident of God's love and provision during times of trial._____

Abide in Christ Total:_____

LIVE IN THE WORD

I regularly read and study my Bible._____

I believe the Bible is God's Word and provides His instructions for life._____

I evaluate cultural ideas and trends by Biblical standards._____

I can answer questions about life and faith from a Biblical perspective._____

I replace impure or inappropriate thoughts with God's truth._____

I demonstrate honesty in my actions and conversation._____

When the Bible exposes an area of my life needing change, I respond to make things right._____

Generally, my public and private self are the same._____
I use the Bible as the guide for the way I think and act._____

I study the Bible to gain direction for daily living._____

Live By God's Word Total:_____

PRAY IN FAITH

My prayers focus on discovering God's will more than expressing my needs._____

I trust God to answer when I pray and wait patiently on His timing._____

My prayers include thanksgiving, praise, confession, and requests._____

I expect to grow in my prayer life and intentionally seek help to improve._____

I spend as much time listening to God as talking to Him._____

I pray because I am aware of my complete dependence on God for everything in my life._____

I believe that weekly prayer group time is important to my prayer life._____

I maintain an attitude of prayer throughout each day._____

I believe my prayers impact my life and the lives of others._____
I engage in a daily prayer time._____

Pray In Faith Total:_____

FELLOWSHIP WITH BELIEVERS

I forgive others when their actions harm me._____

I admit my errors in relationships and humbly seek forgiveness from the one I've hurt._____

I allow other Christians to hold me accountable for spiritual growth._____

I seek to live in harmony with other members of my family._____

I place the interest of others above my self-interest._____

I am gentle and kind in my interactions with others._____

I try to listen to feedback from others to help me discover areas for growth._____

I show patience in my relationships with family and friends._____

I encourage others by pointing out their strengths rather than criticizing their weaknesses._____

My time commitments demonstrate that I value relationships over work/career/hobbies._____

Build Godly Relationships Total: _____

WITNESS TO THE WORLD

I share my faith in Christ with non-believers._____

I regularly pray for non-believers I know._____

I make my faith known to those in my ministry and the unsaved contacts through work._____

I intentionally maintain relationships with non-believers in order to share my testimony.____

When confronted about my faith, I remain consistent and firm in my testimony.____

I help others understand how to effectively share a personal testimony.____

I make sure the people I witness to get the follow-up and support needed to grow in Christ.____

I encourage my church and friends to support mission efforts.____

I am prepared to share my testimony at any time.____

My actions demonstrate a belief in and commitment to the Great Commission (Matthew 28:19-20).____

Witness to the World Total:____

MINISTER TO OTHERS

I understand my spiritual gifts and use those gifts to serve others.____

I serve others expecting nothing in return.____

I sacrificially contribute my finances to help others in my church and community.____

I go out of my way to show love to people I meet.____

Meeting the needs of others is an important part of my giving.____

I share Biblical truth with those I serve as God gives
opportunity.____

I act as if other's needs are as important as my own.____

I expect God to use me every day in His work.____

I regularly contribute time to a ministry at my church.____

I help others identify ministry gifts and become involved in
ministry.____

Minister to Others Total:_____

Your Discipleship Wheel

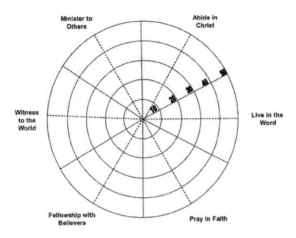

For a visual representation of your spiritual assessment complete
the following steps:

On the dotted line in each discipline section of the circle plot a
point corresponding to your total score for that discipline.
Place similar points on the solid lines to the immediate right
and left of each dotted line.

Connect the plotted points with curved lines similar to the lines of
the circle.

Using a pencil or marker shade the areas in each section between
the lines you drew and the center of the circle. The shaded
areas reveal your personal discipleship wheel at this point in
your spiritual journey.

Ask yourself these questions:

Which areas have the most shading? At this point in your spiritual journey, you see these as the strongest elements of your spiritual growth. List below one benefit these strengths bring to

a. You personally: _____

_____

_____

b. Your family: _____

_____

_____

c. Your church: _____

_____

_____

Which areas have the least shading? At this point in your spiritual life you see these as the areas needing the most improvement. List below one benefit that growth in these disciplines would bring to:

a. You personally: _____

_____

_____

b. Your family: _____

_____

_____

c. Your church: _____

_____

5. Make specific plans to grow spiritually this next year.

_____

_____

_____

Steve Damron

CHAPTER 4
THE PURE LIFE

THE DEVIL'S LIE TO A BELIEVER IS THAT A PURE MIND, PURE THOUGHTS AND A PURE HEART ARE AN IMPOSSIBILITY IN THIS LIFE.

II TIMOTHY 2:22
Flee also youthful lusts: but follow righteousness,
faith, charity, peace, with them that call
on the Lord out of a pure heart.

Purity is becoming a lost commodity in the believer's life. Yet, purity can be had through the work of the Holy Spirit in a Christian's life. My prayer is that this book will challenge that believer that has given up on the concept of living a pure life. God can and wants to give victory. Take God at His word and start living the pure life.

PURITY

The following epitaph was once placed over a soldier's grave:

"Here lies a soldier, whom all must applaud,
Who fought many battles at home and abroad;
But the hottest engagement he ever was in
Was the conquest of self in the battle of sin."

II TIMOTHY 2:20-22

But in a great house there are not only vessels of gold and of silver, but also of wood and of earth; and some to honour, and some to dishonour. If a man therefore purge himself from these, he shall be a vessel unto honour, sanctified, and meet for the master's use, and prepared unto every good work. Flee also youthful lusts: but follow righteousness, faith, charity, peace, with them that call on the Lord out of a pure heart.

We should pay attention to the words of admonition by the Apostle Paul to Timothy who was then in the ministry. He tells this young preacher to purge himself, flee youthful lusts, and be a vessel unto HONOR! Charles Spurgeon, in referencing this passage, mentions, "A man would not go into a plague hospital and inoculate himself with the plague when he knew that 99 of every 100 that took it would die; but you do! No man seeing 20 or 30 men attempting to walk along the face of a cliff, and all falling over and perishing, would follow them; but you do! No man seeing the flame and the furnace heat of the building, and one fireman falling through, and another, hearing the words, "Stand off!" would go in; but you rush in, even though others perished before you. Here are men that think they can go down into the house of death, amid the lures of corruption there, and come out unscathed; you are rotten already! Men think they can play the part of a rascal and be prosperous in life; the halter is around their neck! They think that they can drink, and cast off the danger; they are on the broad road, and not far from infamy! O, slow of heart to believe the testimony of mankind, the testimony of your own experience, and the solemn Word of God!"

It is sobering to think of the many Christians that have taken the unclean path. God wants us to be pure in our walk with the Lord. As we begin this study, pray that God will open up your heart to the Holy Spirit and let Him convict you of this vice that has become a plague in America: Purity!

You may say that in doing this study for Christian young people that I am preaching to the choir. There was a study done in 2013 among so-called Christians. What they found was alarming—they found that 50% of saved men 18 and over had a problem with pornography. These are the men that told the truth about their problem. We can criticize the world for its many vices and wickedness, but we as churches have given up on the idea of purity.

Remember Paul, talking to the Ephesians, said in chapter 5 verse 1-3, "Be ye therefore followers of God, as dear children; And walk in love, as Christ also hath loved us, and hath given himself for us an offering and a sacrifice to God for a sweetsmelling savour. But fornication, and all uncleanness, or covetousness, let it not be once named among you, as becometh saints;"

The story is told of an Arabian princess who was once presented by her teacher with an ivory casket, not to be opened until a year had passed. The time, impatiently waited for, came at last. With trembling haste she unlocked the treasure, and behold—on the satin linings lay a shroud of rust, the form of something beautiful, but the beauty was gone. A slip of parchment contained these words: "Dear pupil, learn a lesson in your life. This trinket, when enclosed, had upon it only a spot of rust. By neglect it has become the useless thing you now behold, only a blot on its pure surroundings. So a little stain on your character will, by inattention and neglect, mar a bright and useful life, and in time leave only the dark shadow of what might have been. Place herein a jewel of gold, and after many years you will find it still as sparkling as ever. So with yourself—treasure up only the pure, the good, and you will be an ornament to society, and a source of true pleasure to yourself and your friends."

The Bible uses many different words to describe purity—one is *sanctification* or *sanctified*.

I CORINTHIANS 6:11

And such were some of you: but ye are washed, but ye are sanctified, but ye are justified in the name of the Lord Jesus, and by the Spirit of our God.

HEBREWS 10:10

By the which will we are sanctified through the offering of the body of Jesus Christ once for all.

HEBREWS 10:14

For by one offering he hath perfected for ever them that are sanctified.

Another word in the Bible that helps us in understanding the concept of purity is the word *holy*.

MATTHEW 7:6

Give not that which is holy unto the dogs, neither cast ye your pearls before swine, lest they trample them under their feet, and turn again and rend you.

ROMANS 12:1

I beseech you therefore, brethren, by the mercies of God, that ye present your bodies a living sacrifice, holy, acceptable unto God, which is your reasonable service.

I CORINTHIANS 3:17

If any man defile the temple of God, him shall God destroy; for the temple of God is holy, which temple ye are.

EPHESIANS 1:4

According as he hath chosen us in him before the foundation of the world, that we should be holy and without blame before him in love.

Purity can have some differing definitions. I think in today's society, we naturally think of morals. There are other ideas to purity. One is that of not being alloyed. What does this mean? An alloyed object is one in which something is added to the pure element. The Bible uses this definition a few times to describe a Christian's purity. The idea is that we are not to be mixed with this world in a spiritual way. In our society, purity is almost a scoffed-at subject. Having morals is something that is part of a by-gone era. Now, as long as you are "safe" in your immoral ventures, then you are not perverted. If you are not married, then there are no moral boundaries; and even now in marriage, we are told to give some flexibility to help each spouse stay faithful. We live in a culture that is vile and corrupt, and this idea of a lack of purity has now even started to creep into our good fundamental churches.

Pornography is big business. According to U.S. News and World Report, the industry five years ago grossed an estimated $10 billion. That figure represents an expenditure of about $30 per person in the United States. That's more than is spent annually on gambling! And it has the same links to organized crime!

Porn is now as American as apple pie, and it has found a place in every corner of our society, including the church. It's now an over $10-billion-dollar-a-year industry in the U.S. alone! This amount is much larger than Hollywood's domestic box office receipts and larger than all the revenues generated by rock and country music recordings. Americans now spend more money at strip clubs than at Broadway shows, off-Broadway shows, or regional, nonprofit theaters, the opera, the ballet, jazz, and classical music performances combined. It is today the #7 grossing industry in the U.S.!

The revenues of the porn industry in the U.S. alone are bigger than the NFL, NBA and Major League Baseball combined. Worldwide porn sales are reported to be $57 billion. To put this in perspective, Microsoft, who sells the operating system used on most of the computers in the world (in addition to other software), reported sales of $36.8 billion in 2004.

As we come to our text in II Timothy, the context is discussing problems in the church. I would like us to look at Biblical purity in our lives, applying it to our hearts and families and how it affects the local church.

PURITY COMES THROUGH SEPARATION

I remember reading of a man who, having a grudge against a railway company, threw a bar of soap into their tank of water. The soap was dissolved and introduced into the boiler, and as soapy water does not generate steam, the engine by and by came to a standstill. The fires were all right, but there was no steam; and we must, figuratively speaking, keep those items out of our lives that will damage the production of good. God cannot use us if we are mixing the wrong materials into our lives. Remember, we owe allegiance to Him who knows every thought of the heart.

Notice what II Timothy 2:21 says in the beginning, "If a man therefore purge himself from these."

The text indicates to us that there are many vessels in the great house. It seems to indicate that even in a church setting you must be careful, because there are those vessels that are bringing honor to the Lord and some vessels to dishonor. For this reason, the Bible instructs us to purge ourselves from these. What does this mean?

We must keep ourselves separate from the world. We must be aware of the worldly influences that are trying to reach us at work, at home, and in our church. We need to be searching our lives continually to be a clean vessel. Most have vessels or containers in their cupboards. If you leave a container to sit for six months, nine months, or one year, will it still be fine to eat or drink out of? You know that it will need to be cleaned from just sitting. In the same way, we need to be continually cleaning our lives so that we are pure vessels and checking for any worldly impurities.

This also means that we should be different. Is it so hard for us to be a peculiar people? Do you hate the looks you get when you are among the world? They think we are Amish or some extreme "cult." Our church has a Christian school, and the kids were all taking a trip to Chicago to watch the Cubs strive to play baseball. It was a large group of 80 people or so, and we took over a large section. One of the fans was overheard asking if our school was an Amish group on an activity. The world should notice a difference in how we talk, dress, and act. It is not always a drastic difference; but as a society becomes more godless, then the differences will be dramatically seen. This is not always comfortable to us as human beings. We love to be liked and want acceptance, but our purity demands a separation from this world and its system. You must not get enamored with the world. Remember the world's plight. Remember the world's end.

When it comes to the world, we must remember that it is at enmity with our Savior, the Lord Jesus Christ. For this reason, we must call out the world and its system as contrary to the Christian way. We must unashamedly stand for godly purity in our lives. The story is told of Antony William Boehme, a German preacher. He once preached from Exodus 20:14, "Thou shalt not commit adultery." A man who was of nobility, who was one of his hearers, felt himself so much insulted that he challenged Boehme to fight a duel, because he thought his sermon was designed entirely to offend him. Boehme accepted the challenge and appeared in his robes; but instead of a pistol he had the Bible in his hand, and spoke to him in the following manner: "I am sorry you were so much offended when I preached against that destructive vice; at the time I did not even think of you. Here I appear with the Sword of the Spirit, and if your conscience condemns you, I beseech you, for your own salvation, to repent of your sins and lead a new life. If you will, then fire at me immediately, for I would willingly lose my life if that might be the means of saving your soul." The chevalier was so struck with this language that he embraced him and solicited his friendship. A bold man was this preacher, and reminds you of another bold man in English history, Hugh Latimer, Bishop of Worcester, who presented to Henry VIII a New Testament for a new year's gift, doubled down at the leaf where is written, "Whoremongers and adulterers God will judge" (Hebrews 13:4). God's truth must be told and not be kept back.

It will never do us any good to play around with the vice of our flesh. Lust does not just mean sensual, although in today's evil world that is about all that the devil has to bring into our path for us to fall. We have become so weak and base as American Christians that the simplest of vices makes us fall into the deepest of sins. Oh! That God would raise a generation that could withstand the pull of this world and would separate themselves unto Him.

Andrew Fuller, after his conversion at 16 years of age, felt that he could no longer participate in the rough merrymaking indulged in on holidays by the young people of his town. So he tells us, "Whenever a feast or holiday occurred, instead of sitting at home with myself, I went to a neighboring village to visit some Christian friend and returned when all was over. By this step I was delivered from those mental participations in folly which had given me so much uneasiness. Thus, the seasons of temptation became to me times of refreshing in the presence of the Lord."

PURITY COMES THROUGH PREPARATION

The word is used in our text, "prepared for every good work." What do we mean by preparing ourselves to be pure? There should be a specific plan, a purpose, to do this.

We have a Bible that can help us prepare for the battle of purity in our lives. I have included some help pages in the back of this book to develop a Biblical plan of Scripture memory, Bible reading, fasting, and praying. Paul told us that the weapons of our warfare are not carnal. We must strengthen ourselves in the Word of God by reading and memorizing its contents. We must become useful with the weapon that God has given us. How much time do you read and memorize the Word of God? This will tell you if you are really serious about overcoming some vice in the area of purity.

We have the availability of the Holy Spirit to guide us into all truth and to teach us what we need to know. I would challenge you to look up verses on the Holy Spirit. There is a lack of Biblical understanding on His ministry and His work in the believer's life. I have talked with many young people who are struggling through depression, disappointment, or despair in some area of their lives and they are trying in their own strength to defeat these foes. The

Holy Spirit can daily lead and guide you, and He desires to be a comforter. That word indicates one who comes alongside. The Holy Spirit wants to be your partner in the battle for purity. A person of the Godhead wants to engage the enemy side by side with you. Victory can be had with a warrior such as this.

So many Christians do not prepare for the battle of purity. They march aimlessly towards the battlefield with no arms ready for battle; no armor to guard against the fiery darts of the wicked. How foolish of us!

There was once an old monk walking through the forest with a little scholar by his side. The old man suddenly stopped and pointed to four plants close at hand. The first was beginning to peep above the ground; the second had rooted itself pretty well into the earth; the third was a small shrub; whilst the fourth and last was a full-sized tree. Then the old monk said to his young companion, "Pull up the first." The youth easily pulled it up with his fingers. "Now pull the second." The youth obeyed, but not so easily. "And the third." But the boy had to put forth all his strength and to use both arms before he succeeded in uprooting it. "And now," said the master, "try your hand upon the fourth." But lo! the trunk of the tall tree, grasped in the arms of the youth, scarcely shook its leaves, and the little fellow found it impossible to tear its roots from the earth. Then the wise old monk explained to his scholar the meaning of the four trials. "This, my son, is just what happens with our passions. When they are young and weak, one may, by a little watchfulness over self, and the help of a little self-denial, easily tear them up; but if we let them cast their roots deep down into our souls, then no human power can uproot them, the Almighty hand of the Creator alone can pluck them out. For this reason, watch well over the first movements of your soul, and study by acts of virtue to keep your passions well in check."

It is vital that we put our flesh in check as soon as we can. When we allow our passions and our lusts to become stronger and stronger over years of relenting to them, they will eventually control our lives. We must do this personally and daily in our lives. Resist the devil; flee from fleshly lust; and keep the world at arm's length. By developing a plan to fight and resist at an early age in your life, you will be developing godly habits. You may not have a problem with pornography—but other secret sins? (shopping; debt spending; overeating, etc.)

HOW TO OVERCOME SECRET SIN:

Confess your sin to another person (James 5:16).
Stand in His forgiveness (1 John 1:9).
Flee temptation; fill up with God (2 Timothy 2:22).
Walk in His power (Galatians 5:16).

PURITY COMES THROUGH DETERMINATION

Notice what our text tells Timothy. He is supposed to be active in fleeing some things. All of the words in the context seem to give the idea of determination. I am determined to purge myself; I am determined to prepare myself to be clean and stay clean, and I am determined to flee some things. The context gives the idea that I am setting some items in place to protect my purity, even much so as to flee things if necessary.

A well-known merchant had a placard nailed to the desk in his office. It said, "WHICH? Wife or whiskey? The babies or the bottles? HEAVEN OR HELL?" To the question of a visitor, he replied, "I wrote that myself. Some time ago I found myself falling into the habit of drinking an occasional glass of whiskey with a friend. Soon my stomach got bad, my faculties dulled, and I had a constant craving for stimulants. I saw tears in the eyes of my wife and wonder on the faces of my children. One day I sat down and wrote that card. As I looked at it, an awful revelation burst upon me like a flash. I nailed it there and read it many times that day. I went home sober that night and have not touched a drop since."

Satan has geared modern technology to offer internet sites, videos, and DVDs that fit with his perfect plan of ruining young men and women in the privacy of their home or the privacy of their phones. Satan's plan is to get all men and women entangled in some form of impurity. No longer does a man need to go into some seedy adult bookstore to view x-rated materials—the so-called adult entertainment industry now pumps the stuff right into our hand-held devices. We need to have the determination to flee from these things. Put filters on your computers, get checks put into place for surfing the internet, and get some accountable reporting to those who love and care for you. We live in a technology age that offers some amazing advantages, but anything left unchecked in human hands will try to find an evil use. This is the nature of man; we have a sin nature. Don't let the good that technology can bring be used by the devil to ruin your purity.

Spurgeon tells of a lady who was trying to hire a coachman. Two or three applicants called to see her about the situation, and in answer to her inquiries, the first applicant said, "Yes, madam, you could not have a better coachman than myself." She replied, "How near do you think you could drive to danger without an accident?" "Madam, I could go within a yard of it, and yet you would be perfectly safe." "Very well," she said, "you will not suit me." The second one had heard the question upon which the other had been rejected, and therefore he was ready with his answer, "Danger! Madam, why I could drive within a hair's breadth, and yet be perfectly safe." "Then you will not suit me at all." When number three came in, he was asked, "Are you a good driver?" "Well," he

replied, "I am careful and have never met with an accident." "But how near do you think you could drive to danger?" "Madam," he said, "that is a thing I never tried. I always drive as far away from danger as ever I can." The lady at once replied, "You are the kind of coachman I want, and I will engage you at once." Get such a coachman as that yourself, to guide your own heart and lead your own character. Do not see how near you can go to sin, but see how far you can keep away from it. (C. H. Spurgeon.)

When we face intense spiritual pressure and anxiety, or when the devil has brought us low with his onslaughts of temptations, we need a plan to strengthen ourselves spiritually. We have developed spiritual boot camp with this in mind. It is not for the spiritually timid soul. It is made with the desire to strengthen and rejuvenate the spiritually down and out. Every Christian goes through times when the powers of darkness or the prince of the power of the air seems to have his every way and whim in our lives. When this occurs, we must take some intense steps to gain back the ground that has been lost. This requires a few considerations for the person who is endeavoring to take this challenge.

First, there must be DETERMINATION. One cannot be an overcomer in the spiritual warfare if there is not some resolution on the part of the believer.

Second, a believer must commit to being FAITHFUL in the effort to defeat the stronghold that seems to easily beset him.

Third, there must be PERSISTENCE in the battle. Many believers talk about trying to overcome a problem, but they do not have the endurance to finish the battle.

Finally, there must be INTEGRITY. It is so important that we hold ourselves accountable to someone when we are trying to overcome an area in our lives. Have the integrity to talk to someone who can help you win the battle.

These four ingredients will help you to take the spiritual workout laid out for you in the following pages and hopefully make the changes that you need to thrive again in your Christian walk.

REVIEW QUESTIONS

1. Paul admonished Timothy to watch out for what things in his life?
2. What do we need to keep ourselves separate from in order to remain pure in our lives?
3. How can we strengthen ourselves in the Word of God?
4. List four steps to help in overcoming sin?
5. What distance should we be from sin?
6. List two bad examples of purity in the Bible and some characteristics that led to their downfall.

7. List two good examples of purity in the Bible and some characteristics that helped them stand against lust.

ADDITIONAL HELPS
FOR THE PURE LIFE

QUOTES TO PONDER CONCERNING PURITY

Either sin will keep you from the Word, or the Word will keep you from sin. ~ John Bunyan

This desire for heart purity is a creation of the Holy Spirit at work in the heart. ~ Duncan Campbell

"He came to deliver us from our sinful dispositions, and create in us pure hearts, and when we have Him with us it will not be hard for us. Then the service of Christ will be delightful." ~ Dwight L. Moody

"I would sooner be holy than happy if the two things could be divorced. Were it possible for a man always to sorrow and yet to be pure, I would choose the sorrow if I might win the purity, for to be free from the power of sin, to be made to love holiness, is true happiness." ~ C.H. Spurgeon

A 30-DAY CHALLENGE FOR SPIRITUAL RENEWAL
The 30-Day Action Plan

The Plan: We will lay out 30 days of Scripture memory, Scripture readings, and Fasting and Prayer requirements. During this time, there must be a commitment to cut away from the influence of the world and its influence. There should be limited contact with the world. We will try to give advice on this.

The Purpose: To give men the ability to strengthen their spiritual walk with the Lord. This will be done by taking 30 days and getting spiritually tough on one's self. The plan is to take 30 days to limit the world, the flesh, and the devil's influence in one's life.

The following are some suggestions that will help as you go through the 30 DAY CHALLENGE:

Do not be discouraged if you are hit with intense temptation. This will be normal. The devil knows that you are trying to be committed to God and increase your devotion to God. The devil will try to get you side-tracked. "Do your best and forget the rest!" Stopping will harm you and will develop a quitting attitude. Doing something is better than doing nothing. The devil knows this, so he wants to just get you to stop.

Realize that there may be a family emergency, work-related disaster, or similar circumstance that will take you away from the plan. You must deal with this situation. Pause on your challenge and take care of the problem, and then resume where you left off. The important thing is to resume and get back at the plan.

There will be a few days to study the Biblical concept of fasting, but this will be after the first day of fasting. In your own personal Bible study, take some time to look up the idea of fasting. We have included some additional articles on fasting if you desire to look at them. It is recommended that the fasting be "food" only fast. Some people do fasting of food and water, but this does not seem to be very healthy. It is up to you to decide which type of fast that you would do, but I recommend a "food" only fast.

At the end of each week, we have space to review the past week and see what God has revealed to you. During this review time, you should look at weaknesses which showed up in your life such as laziness or struggles with self (pride, animosity, anger). God showed you these weaknesses so that you can work on them. Develop a plan to help conquer them over the next weeks during this time that you are analyzing things. You should also review closely what you have learned through Scripture readings and memory.

Try to take a series of days, a set of one or two days in a row, through the 30 days that you can be unplugged from your cellphone and email. This may be hard with work-related items; but the more you can unplug from the world, the better God can get hold of you. You may have to plan a little more in preparation for this by contacting a few people to help you over the day or two that you are trying to "unplug." In these days, you should remove yourself from newspapers, blogs, and news stations. Remember the Psalmist's challenge to "Be still and know that I am God."

We have developed a calendar to help in organizing the 30-day plan. The calendar starts on Sunday, but it can be adapted to start on any day. Modify the calendar to fit into your schedule, and then keep to the plan.

MEMORY VERSES TO HELP A LIFE TO BE PURE

Sunday	Monday	Tuesday	Wednesday	Thursday	Friday	Saturday
Bible-Reading Week	Readings on Prayer Life	1 Hour of Bible Reading	Readings on Bible Study	1 Hour of Bible Reading	Readings on Quiet Time	1 Hour of Prayer
Week 1 Review						
Scripture-Memory Week	Readings on Prayer Life	30 minutes of Memory Verse Work	Readings on Bible Study	1 Hour of Bible Reading	Fast Day	Readings on Quiet Time
Week 2 Review						
Purity Week	Readings on Purity	30 minutes of Memory Verse Work	Readings on Purity	Readings on Purity	Readings on Purity	1 Hour of Prayer
Week 3 Review						
Prayer & Fasting Week	Study on Fasting	1 Hour of Bible Reading	Study on Fasting 1 Hour of Prayer	Fast Day	Fast Day	30 Minutes of Memory Verse Work
Week 4 Review						
Review Day	Review Day	FINISHED!				

I JOHN 1:4-10

And these things write we unto you, that your joy may be full. This then is the message which we have heard of him, and declare unto you, that God is light, and in him is no darkness at all. If we say that we have fellowship with him, and walk in darkness, we lie, and do not the truth: But if we walk in the light, as he is in the light, we have fellowship one with another, and the blood of Jesus Christ his Son cleanseth us from all sin. If we say that we have no sin, we deceive ourselves, and the truth is not in us. If we confess our sins, he is faithful and just to forgive us our sins, and to cleanse us from all unrighteousness. If we say that we have not sinned, we make him a liar, and his word is not in us.

PSALM 1:1-6

Blessed is the man that walketh not in the counsel of the ungodly, nor standeth in the way of sinners, nor sitteth in the seat of the scornful. But his delight is in the law of the LORD; and in his law doth he meditate day and night. And he shall be like a tree planted by the rivers of water, that bringeth forth his fruit in his season; his leaf also shall not wither; and whatsoever he doeth shall prosper. The ungodly are not so: but are like the chaff which the wind driveth away. Therefore the ungodly shall not stand in the judgment, nor sinners in the congregation of the righteous. For the LORD knoweth the way of the righteous: but the way of the ungodly shall perish.

ROMANS 6:6-16

Knowing this, that our old man is crucified with him, that the body of sin might be destroyed, that henceforth we should not serve sin. For he that is dead is freed from sin. Now if we be dead with Christ, we believe that we shall also live with him: Knowing that Christ being raised from the dead dieth no more; death hath no more dominion over him. For in that he died, he died unto sin once: but in that he liveth, he liveth unto God. Likewise reckon ye also yourselves to be dead indeed unto sin, but alive unto God through Jesus Christ our Lord. Let not sin therefore reign in yourmortal body, that ye should obey it in the lusts thereof. Neither yield ye your members as instruments of unrighteousness unto sin: but yield yourselves unto God, as those that are alive from the dead, and your members as instruments of righteousness unto

God. For sin shall not have dominion over you: for ye are not under the law, but under grace. What then? shall we sin, because we are not under the law, but under grace? God forbid. Know ye not, that to whom ye yield yourselves servants to obey, his servants ye are to whom ye obey; whether of sin unto death, or of obedience unto righteousness?

ROMANS 8:1-4

There is therefore now no condemnation to them which are in Christ Jesus, who walk not after the flesh, but after the Spirit. For the law of the Spirit of life in Christ Jesus hath made me free from the law of sin and death. For what the law could not do, in that it was weak through the flesh, God sending his own Son in the likeness of sinful flesh, and for sin, condemned sin in the flesh: That the righteousness of the law might be fulfilled in us, who walk not after the flesh, but after the Spirit.

THE EMPEROR'S SEEDS
WAYNE RICE

Once there was an emperor in the Far East who was growing old and knew the time was coming to choose his successor. Instead of choosing one of his assistants or one of his own children, he decided to do something different.

He called all the young people in the kingdom together one day. He said, "It has come time for me to step down and to choose the next emperor. I have decided to choose one of you." The kids were shocked! But the emperor

106

continued. "I am going to give each one of you a seed today. One seed. It is a very special seed. I want you to go home, plant the seed, water it, and come back here one year from today with what you have grown from this one seed. I will then judge the plants that you bring to me, and the one I choose will be the next emperor of the kingdom!"

There was one boy named Ling who was there that day and he, like the others, received a seed. He went home and excitedly told his mother the whole story. She helped him get a pot and some planting soil, and he planted the seed and watered it carefully. Every day he would water it and watch to see if it had grown.

After about three weeks, some of the other youths began to talk about their seeds and the plants that were beginning to grow. Ling kept going home and checking his seed, but nothing ever grew. Three weeks, four weeks, five weeks went by. Still nothing.

By now others were talking about their plants, but Ling didn't have a plant, and he felt like a failure. Six months went by, still nothing in Ling's pot. He just knew he had killed his seed. Everyone else had trees and small plants, but he had nothing. Ling didn't say anything to his friends, however. He just kept waiting for his seed to grow.

A year finally went by and all the youths of the kingdom brought their plants to the emperor for inspection. Ling told his mother that he wasn't going to take an empty pot. But she encouraged him to go, and take his pot, and to be honest about what happened. Ling felt sick to his stomach, but he knew his mother was right. He took his empty pot to the palace.

When Ling arrived, he was amazed at the variety of plants grown by all the other youths. They were beautiful, in all shapes and sizes. Ling put his empty pot on the floor and many of the other kids laughed at him. A few felt sorry for him and just said, "Hey, nice try."

When the emperor arrived, he surveyed the room and greeted the young people. Ling just tried to hide in the back. "My, what great plants, trees and flowers you have grown," said the emperor. "Today, one of you will be appointed the next emperor!"

All of a sudden, the emperor spotted Ling at the back of the room with his empty pot. He ordered his guards to bring him to the front.

Ling was terrified. "The emperor knows I'm a failure! Maybe he will have me killed!" When Ling got to the front, the emperor asked his name. "My name is Ling," he replied. All the kids were laughing and making fun of him. The emperor asked everyone to quiet down. He looked at Ling, and then announced to the crowd, "Behold your new emperor! His name is Ling!"

Ling couldn't believe it. Ling couldn't even grow his seed. How could he be the new emperor?

Then the emperor said, "One year ago today, I gave everyone here a seed. I told you to take the seed, plant it, water it, and bring it back to me today. But I gave you all boiled seeds which would not grow. All of you, except Ling, have brought me trees and plants and flowers. When you found that the seed would not grow, you substituted another seed for one I gave you. Ling was the only one with the courage and honesty to bring me a pot with my seed in it. Therefore, he is the one who will be the new emperor!"

(From *More Hot Illustrations for Youth Talks*)

THE FLAT TIRE
WAYNE RICE

Two students were taking organic chemistry at the university. Having done well in their work and labs, they were both going into the final exam with solid A's. So far, so good. Trouble was, they were so confident that they decided to party the night before the big test. It was a great night; one thing led to another, and they ended up sleeping late the following morning.

They missed the exam! Disasterville! Being inventive souls, though, they went to see the professor to explain that they had been visiting a sick, out-of-town friend the night before. On the way home they had a flat tire. With no spare tire and no car jack, they were stranded. They could only manage to hitch a lift back to town midmorning, which is why they missed the test. They were really sorry to have missed the exam, they said (they were so looking forward to it!), but wondered whether they might be able to take it that afternoon.

The professor thought about it for a moment and decided that this would be permissible, since they hadn't had time to discuss the exam with any of the students who had already taken it. After a short break for lunch, the two students were ready for the test. The professor placed them in separate rooms, handed each of them an exam booklet, and told them to begin.

Page one, question one. A simple one for five points. This will be easy! Having answered the first question each of the students turned the page for question number two: It read: "Which tire?" (95 points).

(From Still *More Hot Illustrations for Youth Talks*)

Every Day is a Tough Day

Steve Damron

CHAPTER 5
THE TEMPERATE LIFE

BEING FORCED TO WORK, AND FORCED TO DO YOUR BEST, WILL BREED IN YOU TEMPERANCE AND SELF-CONTROL, DILIGENCE AND STRENGTH OF WILL, CHEERFULNESS AND CONTENT, AND A HUNDRED VIRTUES WHICH THE IDLE WILL NEVER KNOW.

I CORINTHIANS 9:27
But I keep under my body, and bring it into subjection: lest that by any
means, when I have preached to others,
I myself should be a castaway.

Many of the problems that Christians get into are caused by lack of being temperate and practicing NOT self-control, but Christ-control. Discipline is an important, but often neglected, part of the Christian life. Many broken friendships, and many harsh words come, as a result of not learning how to be temperate. Too many Christians take the attitude that they cannot control their temper, their thoughts, or their actions. This is simply not true. With God's Holy Spirit help we can practice temperance.

TEMPERANCE

There was once a king who desired to have it all. He desired riches more than anything in the world. One day his dream came true. You have heard of it, "The Midas Touch," when everything the man touched turned to gold. He ran to the coffee table; he ran to the chair; he ran to the bed; he could not stop touching things—the sight of gold exhilarated him. He thought of everything he could get his hands on. He sat down to eat in the evening, grabbed an apple, and it turned to gold. He laughed with glee.

It was just about bedtime, and his daughter came running to him "Daddy, Daddy!" She jumped into his arms and there she remained frozen as gold. What was so good turned out to be rotten, and this is what happens to us if we do not have self-control or Biblical temperance in our lives. The good in this life will be spoiled.

THE BIBLICAL DEFINITION OF TEMPERANCE

The Bible uses the term temperance in a number of passages. Let's consider a few of them.

"But the fruit of the Spirit is love, joy, peace, longsuffering, gentleness, goodness, faith, meekness, temperance: against such there is no law" (Galatians 5:22, 23).

According to this passage, evidence of the Holy Spirit is manifested through a person's behavior. It is one of the fruits of the Spirit. It is one of the Christian graces that we are to grow in: "...add to your faith virtue; and to virtue knowledge; and to knowledge temperance..." (II Peter 1:5-6).

Strong's Concordance gives the Greek word for temperance as the following: egkrateia. It means simply, self-control (especially continence). In other words, it is self-discipline.

When you think about the word "discipline," there are probably several different things that come to mind. To a child, it probably means getting a spanking for doing something he shouldn't have done. To a soldier, discipline means conforming to the regulations, obedience to orders, KP duty, and reveille on cold mornings. To a student, discipline means a class with a lot of work and exams. To a church member, church discipline means voting someone out of the church that has broken their word in their covenant or in their behavior as a Christian.

And all of these are correct. All of these are aspects of discipline. However these things are examples of imposed discipline in which one person or group forces or pushes another person to follow or obey. A parent disciplines his child to teach him obedience. The Army disciplines the soldier to teach strict obedience. A school disciplines by making students do the work. The church disciplines in order to encourage members to remain faithful. It is imposed discipline. So, when we turn the idea to ourselves, we are talking about putting disciplines into place to control our "self." It is putting disciplines into place such as a parent or school would in order to allow "self" to be able to accomplish the work that God has given us to do.

The Greek word for temperance means self-control. Why is self-control so important in a believer's life? We don't have anybody telling us what we have to do to live the Christian life. For instance, a Christian does not have anybody telling him how many hours a week to read his Bible; nor anybody making him attend all the church services at his church; nor anybody telling him how much time to spend in prayer; nor anybody following him around making sure that his light is shining in this dark world; nor anybody telling him how much money he should be giving to the church. The list could go on and on regarding a believer's personal holiness. There's only one thing that will keep a believer from doing wrong and living a self-centered life. It is the development of temperance or self-control through the ministry work of the Holy Spirit.

It takes a lot more character to have the self-discipline to do something on your own than it does to be told what to do, when to do it, and how to do it.

A BIBLICAL EXAMPLE OF TEMPERANCE

"Know ye not that they which run in a race run all, but one receiveth the prize? So run, that ye may obtain. And every man that striveth for the mastery is temperate in all things. Now they do it to obtain a corruptible crown; but we an incorruptible. I therefore so run, not as uncertainly; so fight I, not as one that beateth the air: But I keep under my body, and bring it into subjection: lest that by any means, when I have preached to others, I myself should be a castaway" (I Corinthians 9:24-27).

The Apostle Paul was very much concerned about disciplining his own life. In the passage listed above, Paul uses the illustration of an athletic contest—a race. That was a familiar thing to these

Christians in Corinth. The Greeks had two great athletic events—the Olympic games with which we are very much familiar, and the Isthmian games which were held at the city of Corinth every three years. In fact, if you go to Corinth, you can still see the areas where the races were run. The starting blocks where the athletes began the races are still embedded in the stones. Paul uses this figure because, to him, the Christian life is similar to races at these games.

These Corinthians knew that every athlete who participated in the races had to take an oath that they had been training for 10 months and that they had given up certain foods in their diet to enable them to endure the race. They subjected themselves to rather rigorous discipline in order to win, and yet Paul says all that they were winning was a "corruptible crown." In other words, they were running for a reward that over time would fade. It was traditionally a pine wreath, but in contrast, the Apostle Paul says that we are running for "an incorruptible" crown, one that is of an eternal nature.

Paul sees life this way. Our aim is to run the race of life in order to be a useful instrument of God; to be used whenever and wherever He wants to use us. That was Paul's objective. When he woke up in the morning, it was first in his thoughts; it is what set the tone of his day. He was ready to give up certain indulgences, if necessary, which may have been perfectly right and proper for him at a given time. But if they interfered with his objective to be what God wanted him to be, Paul said he would be happy to give them up. For him the great objective was to win the prize and to feel the sense of delight that he was being used by God.

In this picture of running a race that Paul uses, it is obvious you cannot do this without self-discipline. There is always something in life that will distract you if you let it. There are temptations to turn aside, to give up, to sit back and let life go on and enjoy yourself. All these things will sabotage your Christian effectiveness. That's what Paul is talking about. And so he says we need self-discipline; we need self-control.

It has been said that discipline is what we need the most in our modern world and what we want the least. So we have a country filled with students dropping out of school, husbands and wives looking for divorces, employees walking out on their jobs and Christians who are becoming unfaithful. Many of them simply don't have the self-discipline that it takes to see their problems through. They run from their problems, look for the easy way out, and quit when the going gets rough.

Solomon once said, "If thou faint in the day of adversity, thy strength is small" (Proverbs 24:10). Days of adversity are going to come. We need to understand that and develop the self-discipline to handle them.

To help us understand the concept of self-control better, I want us to look at another verse. It is found in Proverbs 16:32, "He that is slow to anger is better than the mighty; and he that ruleth his spirit than he that taketh a city." This gives us a very basic definition that self-control is "ruling your spirit." In this portion of Scripture the Bible compares self-control with one who conquers a city, and states that one who can practice self-control is better than one who can overthrow a city.

Throughout history the world has made much out of military victories. From ancient times we have records of generals and the cities that they have conquered. As we move through time we tend to make heroes out of generals. I think of two men who became presidents not because of their political abilities but because they were great soldiers—Dwight Eisenhower and Ulysses Grant. We give our warriors the highest honor and greatest power. But here in Proverbs 16:32 we are reminded that the simple, private victory of living in self-control is greater than all the great victories of any war. Let us consider why this is so.

In ancient times before the invention of artillery and heavy ordnance, to lay siege to a city took a lot of energy, time, and manpower. It took Nebuchadnezzar, who had by far the strongest army at this time, a year and a half to take the relatively small city of Jerusalem.

A few hundred years later, it took the mighty army of Rome years to accomplish the same feat. But, the battle of self-control is even greater.

It is greater because the enemy is within. The battle of self-control is not an external battle but an internal one. The war of the soul is a civil war. It is a war between our flesh and our spiritual nature.

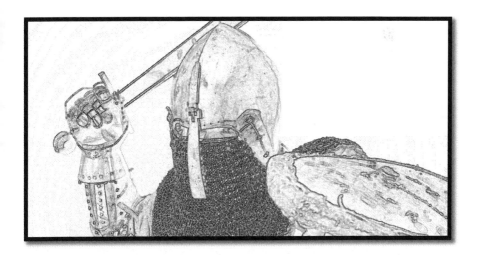

Paul speaks of this inner battle in Galatians 5:17, "For the flesh lusteth against the Spirit, and the Spirit against the flesh; and these are contrary the one to the other: so that ye cannot do the things that ye would." For the Christian there is the battle in the soul to do what is right and to do what is pleasing to the Lord. If you do not have this civil war in you then more than likely you do not have the Holy Spirit in you.

It is also greater because the enemy is unpredictable and cannot be tamed. In ancient times some races of people were harder to rule than others. Some would take defeat very easily while others would fight until the last man was dead. Let us realize that the enemy that we fight in the battle of self-control will not quit until it is dead. The battle between our flesh and the Spirit will continue all the days of our lives. There will be no treaty, NO peace until we get to heaven. The flesh will continue to strive to pull us away from God, to lead us down the roads of temptation and sin. Our sinful nature will be totally put to death when we are glorified in Heaven with Jesus Christ our Lord.

Self-control also requires a greater effort than storming a city because the enemy has great power at times. And the enemy, which is our flesh, is given that power by the one who is trying to defeat it.

Can you imagine a general shipping arms and ammunition to the enemy? Yet that is what we do with our own old, fleshly nature. We give to it what it needs to hinder our spiritual nature. We feed it through our own sin, giving in to its desires and lusts. We give in to the flesh until we have built strongholds in our lives. And it is our fleshly nature that dwells in those strongholds, waiting for us to try and defeat it.

It also takes a greater effort because the enemy that we are dealing with is subtle. What does Jeremiah 17:9 tells us "The heart is deceitful above all things, and desperately wicked; who can know it?"

Let's realize that our flesh is always in the state of plotting treason against us. When all looks safe, that is when it will strike. Our own hearts are deceitful. It will lie to you because it is tainted with sin. It is desperately wicked; prone to turn us from God. Our flesh strives to have us ignore the Word of God and follow the desires of that wicked heart—the lusts of the flesh in our thoughts, in our actions, and in our words. Yet, we can defeat our deceitful heart. We can destroy those strongholds and destroy those walls. And we can begin that by practicing self-control.

HELPS FOR IMPLEMENTING TEMPERANCE INTO A BELIEVER'S LIFE

The story is told of a drunken man who entered his row boat one night to cross the river. He picked up the oars and pulled away—so he thought. He rowed all night but did not reach the destination. When daylight came, he was surprised to find that he was just where he started the night before. He had forgotten to untie his boat. So it is with many of the Lord's followers. They are tied to their habits, desires, wills, or some cherished idol or idols of the heart. Consequently, their lives are fruitless.

Let's consider the acronym—CONTROL, to give us the helps to implement a Biblical control of our flesh.

COMMIT YOUR WAYS TO THE LORD

We have two sets of verses to consider with this idea in mind. The first is found in the book of Psalms.

"Trust in the LORD, and do good; so shalt thou dwell in the land, and verily thou shalt be fed. Delight thyself also in the LORD; and he shall give thee the desires of thine heart. Commit thy way unto the LORD; trust also in him; and he shall bring it to pass" (Psalm 37:3-5).

We see three actions that are referenced in Psalm 37: trusting, delighting and committing. The three actions will work together in helping one overcome weaknesses in the flesh. We must first trust the Lord and do good. There are right actions that must be taken by a young man or young lady. Sometimes, a young person does not understand all the reasoning behind a rule or a caution that adults have put in place in regards to the fleshly appetites. As a young person, trust the Lord and the authority that He has put over you.

The next step is delighting in the Lord. This is contrary to the flesh. A young person must start the process of developing an appetite for the things of God. How does a young person develop a strong walk with the Lord? One way this is done is by faithful attendance to church, to church functions and to those organized activities that will help develop a yearning for the things of God. The world has so much activity that is trying to pull us away from God, so a young person should learn to rely on God-given authority that is working to create God-honoring activity. A young person then needs to work at developing a personal walk with the Lord. This may require some help from the authority put into a young person's life, so don't be afraid to ask your parents, your teachers, or your pastors. They are put there by God to guide and direct your spiritual walk. A young person must learn what Bible study means, Bible memorization, and the proper prayer pattern. These are foreign to our flesh, and our flesh does not like to be spiritual, so a young person must realize that this will be difficult at first.

"The preparations of the heart in man, and the answer of the tongue, is from the LORD. All the ways of a man are clean in his own eyes; but the LORD weigheth the spirits. Commit thy works unto the LORD, and thy thoughts shall be established" (Proverbs 16:1-3).

This second set of verses help us to understand a few more ideas in regards to committing our ways to the Lord. The first is found in understanding that the Lord knows our hearts better than we do. There are times that a young person will say that they are completely right with the Lord, but the Lord knows the heart and is leading the authority in a young person's life to look at some things that seem to be haywire. The next idea is seen in verse 3. We must be willing to cast our lives on the Lord's altar and remove our hands off of the steering wheel. When we commit our ways and actions to the Lord, God will step in to help establish our thought life. There are many young folks who want God to step in and change their thoughts, but they are not willing for the Lord to direct all of their steps. Full surrender is required for God to truly be able to help a Christian believer.

OBSTRUCT AREAS OF YOUR LIFE ON OCCASION

"But I keep under my body, and bring it into subjection: lest that by any means, when I have preached to others, I myself should be a castaway" (I Corinthians 9:27).

In considering this verse, we see that the Apostle Paul was in the habit of keeping his body under. We are not abdicating a return to self-afflicting beating methods. This practice of self-denial was common in the middle ages and was supposed to help someone learn to deny themselves. However, it is a good practice to learn to say no to your desires once in a while. In America, it has grown to be customary to give a child any desire they want and the child then never has heard the word, "No!" The child grows up thinking that the world serves at their pleasure and when someone such as authority decides that the class or the group is going to do something contrary to this entitled child, the child throws a fit saying that they are being denied their rights. As a Christian young person, we must learn that self-denial is part of becoming a strong, mature Christian.

Christians should make it a practice to learn to be disciplined in their life with the things of this world that seem to get "clingy" to their lives. For instance, it is not uncommon for a young man or young woman to be so consumed with an artist that plays Christian or classical music that they cannot seem to study, play, or even enjoy leisure time without that artist's music being played. The young person should restrict their playing of that music for a little while. Why? Because a Christian tries to follow the Biblical example of the Apostle Paul, not being brought under the power of any. Is the artist wrong or sinful? No, but the flesh is trying to get hold in that young person's life by making him dependent on the music instead of a walk with the Lord. Many a young person has been trapped into the mundane of this world by the worldly allure of petty amusements and trinkets which will never bring true happiness. Video games, worldly fashions, popular fads and catchy lingo have all pulled young people into pettiness and an unmeaning purpose of life. Young and older folks need to be in the habit of limiting the world's influence so on occasion live without something that is non-essential. Christians who practices this will find that this weakens the world's grip on their lives.

NEVER GIVE UP

"If thou faint in the day of adversity, thy strength is small. If thou forbear to deliver them that are drawn unto death, and those that are ready to be slain; If thou sayest, Behold, we knew it not; doth not he that pondereth the heart consider it? and he that keepeth thy soul, doth not he know it? and shall not he render to every man according to his works?" (Proverbs 24:10-12).

In the Bible you will find some folks that fainted when things seemed dark, but they did not give up on God and they kept going for the Lord. Let's consider three examples in the Bible of folks who fainted.

1.   Moses—fainted because of the people he was ministering to.

My service is to the Lord. Don't let the folks you are ministering to get you side-tracked with discouragement. There will be times when those that you are trying to show compassion towards will turn on you and they almost hate and despise the work that you are doing. Christ warned His disciples of this when He said that if they hated Him they would hate the disciples also. Christ was trying to help the disciples to understand that Biblical compassion is not always appreciated, but we still are supposed to minister as unto the Lord.

2.   Elijah—Fainted because of outside persecution.

Don't let this world and the negativity of this world get you so down that you are willing to cash it in. Elijah had already seen some amazing answers to prayer as he came down off of Mount Carmel, but the wicked world turned this glorious victory into a discouraging moment for Elijah. He scampered away, but praise the Lord, the Lord found Elijah and fed and nourished him. There are times that as a Christian, you will be overwhelmed by the world's hatred of right and lifting up of wrong. Fainting may occur, but look to the Lord and get the nourishment you need at the brook.

3.   Peter—Fainted because of external circumstances and internal weakness

There are two instances that we find in the Gospels. The one was while the disciples were in the boat on the Sea of Galilee and a great tempest came and was threatening to upheave the boat. Peter looked out and saw Christ walking on the water and called to Christ.

Peter eventually came out, and then he lifted his eyes from off of Christ to the storm that was surrounding him. Instantly, Peter was sinking, but Peter showed us a great truth for us all. He realized his mistake, called out to Christ, and was restored from sinking.

The second time that we see Peter fainting was during the trial of Christ. Peter followed from afar and found himself warming by a fire. Some took note of this man who was unfamiliar, but recognition started to dawn on a few of the folks that were warming themselves. They questioned Peter about his association with the man who was on trial. Peter fainted internally at this point because of the fear that whelmed up in his soul. He denied the Lord who he had grown to love so much over the past few years. In both cases there was a fainting that occurred in the life of Peter.

3 HELPS AGAINST NEVER GIVING UP

1.   Don't Quit Working

"I went by the field of the slothful, and by the vineyard of the man void of understanding; And, lo, it was all grown over with thorns, and nettles had covered the face thereof, and the stone wall thereof was broken down. Then I saw, and considered it well: I looked upon it, and received instruction. Yet a little sleep, a little slumber, a little folding of the hands to sleep: So shall thy poverty come as one that travelleth; and thy want as an armed man" (Proverbs 24:30-34).

What we find in the above-mentioned passage is that laziness is never an option in the Christian life. We may have some times that are hard in our lives and the trials seem to indicate that there is a legitimate reason to not pursue God's calling in our life with diligence. However, God's Word tells us to keep faithful in our daily walk and our daily tasks. When adversity or hard times come in your life, keep focused on the work God has for you. Don't quit working.

2.   Don't Stay Down

"For a just man falleth seven times, and riseth up again: but the wicked shall fall into mischief" (Proverbs 24:16).

Through the pages of Scripture, there are numerous examples of folks who fainted and stayed down and folks who fainted and got up and continued on for God. Fainting in adversity may happen, but a just man or a good man or woman gets up, understanding that their life and service to the Lord is not at an end.

3.   Don't Forget to Go to God

"If thou sayest, Behold, we knew it not; doth not he that pondereth the heart consider it? and he that keepeth thy soul, doth not he know it? and shall not he render to every man according to his works?" (Proverbs 24:12).

It is interesting that this passage is aligned with the verses proceeding. Many times in the book of Proverbs it is hard to find a contextual line. It is often the best approach when looking at the book of Proverbs to do a topical study for this reason. However, these few verses seem to have a string that ties them together— fainting in adversity. The Word of God tells the Christian to remember that God is in control and He will eventually bring all things to light. A Christian lives in this world, but must keep the eternal in view at all times.

Begun in 1869, the Brooklyn Bridge was the dream of German immigrant, John Roebling. Roebling died as construction was beginning and the project was taken over by his wife and his son, Washington, who took over the family business.

To lay the foundations for the bridge, huge caissons (underground cavities) were sunk to the bottom of the East River and pumped dry. Within these manmade caverns, workmen dug the foundation for the bridge's two great towers. Working at such a depth, many men suffered from the bends. In spite of his own poor health, Roebling would go down to inspect the work, twice collapsing in agony. Then the weight of the unprecedented project wore down Roebling's nerves. His condition confined him to his bed for the next ten years. Due to his condition, Roebling could hardly write and barely read, yet he monitored construction from his bed using a telescope, looking through the window of his bedroom of his home a quarter mile away. Roebling dictated his instructions to his wife, Emily, who carried them out. So physically and mentally drained was Roebling that he could not even attend the bridge's opening celebration on May 24, 1883. A grateful President Chester Arthur led a delegation to the engineer's home to thank him personally.

But this remarkable man was not "washed up." With the bridge complete, Washington Roebling fought his way back to health and successfully ran the family business until his death in 1926.

Keep on in spite of your feelings or frustrations.
Keep on though you have been forgotten as was Joseph.
Keep on though you have been forsaken as was Jesus.
Keep on though you have failed as did Peter.
Keep on in spite of fears and foes as did Paul.
Keep on though thrown in the fire as were the three Hebrew children.
Keep on through all the pain, knowing your labor is not in vain!

TURN YOUR EYES UPON JESUS

We referenced the story of Peter on the Sea of Galilee. Let's continue to think of this incident in the life of Peter in regards to our eyes getting out of focus. The story is recorded in both Mark and Luke.

There are some admirable traits that we find with the Apostle Peter. He was bold in stepping out for the Lord. He displayed a great deal of faith in certain instances such as stepping out of the boat on the Sea of Galilee. He was willing to give up all for the cause of Christ, even to go to "war" as in the case of Malchus at the garden of Gethsemane. These are characteristics that are very admirable.

However, we find that the storm that came suddenly on the Sea of Galilee made Peter look away from the person of Christ. This mistake made him start to "go under" the waves of the sea. This same mistake is made often in both young and older folks. They get caught up in the storms or circumstances that seem to be sweeping over their vessel. They then turn to other helps except the obvious help which is Christ in front of them. When it comes to our flesh and the control that a Christian needs to put in place, there is no better person to run to than the person of Jesus Christ. "He was in all points tempted like we were and yet without sin" (Hebrews 4:15). Christ, when leaving this earth, cared so much for us as Christians that He promised to leave a Comforter. That comforter literally means someone who comes alongside. This means that as a Christian, we have someone who will help us become temperate. Turn to Christ and beg again for His mercy and grace to help in time of need.

It is easy for us who profess to be faithful followers of Christ to get caught up in the "things of earth," so that our vision here on this earth becomes the focus and not a heavenly vision of the eternal. This can even happen when we are active in our service to the Lord in serving Him. We become so involved in merely doing outward actions for God that we miss the blessing of personal fellowship with Christ Himself and the Holy Spirit in our daily lives.

I've seen the face of Jesus. He smiled in love on me;
It filled my heart with rapture, my soul with ecstasy.
The scars of deepest anguish were lost in glory bright;
I've seen the face of Jesus. It was a wondrous sight!
Oh, glorious face of beauty, oh gentle touch of care;
If here it is so blessed, what will it be up there? ~Selected

REPLACE SELF-CONTROL WITH GOD CONTROL

Ultimately, controlling ourselves is about being controlled by Christ. When "the love of Christ controls us" (II Corinthians 5:14), when we embrace the truth that he is our sovereign, and God has "left nothing outside his control" (Hebrews 2:8), we can bask in the freedom that we need not muster our own strength to exercise self-control, but we can find strength in the strength of another. In the person of Jesus, "the grace of God has appeared ..." training us—not just "to renounce ungodliness and worldly passions," but "to live self-controlled, upright, and godly lives in the present age" (Titus 2:11–12). Christian temperance is not finally about bringing our bodily emotions and tendencies under our own control, but placing our bodies under the control of Christ by the power of His Spirit.

The Bible indicates to all believers in II Peter that we are to grow in our maturity as believers on this earth. One of the items that we are supposed to add to our faith is temperance or self-control. Christ gives us a great example of a life that had this temperance as a part of the Spirit-filled life. All Christ's life was "without sin" (Hebrews 4:15). The Bible says in I Peter 2: 22, "He committed no sin, neither was deceit found in his mouth." Christ steadied His emotions even when sweat came like drops of blood (Luke 22:44). The Bible says that Christ could have called twelve legions of angels (Matthew 26:53), but he had the stamina to not rebut the false charges (Matthew 27:14) or defend himself (Luke 23:9). When reviled, he did not revile in return (I Peter 2:23). They spit in his face and struck him, slapped him and scourged him (Matthew 27:26,27). In every trial and temptation, "he learned obedience through what he suffered" (Hebrews 5:8), and at the pinnacle of his self-control He was "obedient to the point of death, even death on a cross" (Philippians 2:8). And He is the one who strengthens us (I Timothy 1:12; Philippians 4:13).

In Jesus, we have a source for true self-control far beyond that of our feeble selves. As a believer, a Christian should turn their emotions over to the leading of the Spirit.

OBEY THE SPIRIT'S LEADING

"So then they that are in the flesh cannot please God. But ye are not in the flesh, but in the Spirit, if so be that the Spirit of God dwell in you. Now if any man have not the Spirit of Christ, he is none of his. And if Christ be in you, the body is dead because of sin; but the Spirit is life because of righteousness. But if the Spirit of him that raised up Jesus from the dead dwell in you, he that raised up Christ from the dead shall also quicken your mortal bodies by his Spirit that dwelleth in you. Therefore, brethren, we are debtors, not to the flesh, to live after the flesh. For if ye live after the flesh, ye shall die: but if ye through the Spirit do mortify the deeds of the body, ye shall live. For as many as are led by the Spirit of God, they are the sons of God" (Romans 8:8-14).

This passage is preceded by two chapters in the book of Romans that discuss the effects of sin and the freedom that Christ brought through the death and resurrection. Romans 6:1 tells us that we should not continue in sin. The quandary is then discussed by the Apostle Paul where he then reveals his frustration at the end of chapter 7 saying that the things he wants to do he does not do and the things that he should not do, he does. The Apostle Paul does not leave us hopeless, though. He continues the discussion in chapter 8, where he reveals to us the secret of defeating this old nature; it is found in obeying the Holy Spirit's leading. Remember another writing of the Apostle to the church in Galatia where he said, "This I say then, Walk in the Spirit and ye shall not fulfill the lust of the flesh." The obeying of the Holy Spirit's leading must not be a one-time event. Daily and each moment, a Christian must be submitted to the leading of the Holy Spirit. Through His leading and conviction, a Christian can be temperate. Remember also in Galatians that Paul lists one of the fruits of the Holy Spirit in one's life as temperance.

LIMIT YOUR FLESH'S INFLUENCE

"For though we walk in the flesh, we do not war after the flesh: (For the weapons of our warfare are not carnal, but mighty through God to the pulling down of strong holds;) Casting down imaginations, and every high thing that exalteth itself against the knowledge of God, and bringing into captivity every thought to the obedience of Christ" (II Corinthians 10:3-5).

When a Christian finds that something is taking hold of them, they need to get away from the influence that is exerting itself on their Christian life. A classic example that illustrates this mindset is a man that God saves from the grip of alcoholism. If this man continues to go to the places where he was served alcohol and orders

milk, he is asking to fall again into the trap of alcohol. The man should stay far away from bars and the institutions that influence him to want alcohol. In the same fashion, Christians will

have fleshly tendencies that are stronger at times in their lives. Limit the influence by steering clear of places and venues that seem to heighten the strength of the flesh.

True greatness is found in the man who has lived his life for Christ. A great man is one who has not been overcome by the desires of the flesh, a man who has battled his own sinful nature and has won. What does Christ say in Matthew 16:26? "For what does it profit a man if he gains the whole world, and loses his own soul? Or what will a man give in exchange for his soul?"

The man who is truly great in character is not one who has conquered the world, but one who has conquered his own soul. True character is not found in physical battles won, while losing your soul. This type of earthly grandeur is temporal and will be seen as such in eternity's perspective. True character is found in the man who has battled himself and won, and who has gained a place in heaven through Jesus Christ.

The term "self-control" can be a little confusing. However, the term that we have looked at does not refer to the power we have in and of ourselves, but it refers to the power that we have in Christ through the working of the Holy Spirit that was left for us here on this earth until we are taken to glory. This power is alive and at work in every born-again Christian. God tells us in His word in I John 4:4, "Ye are of God, little children, and have overcome them: because greater is he that is in you, than he that is in the world."

A 23 year old lightweight wrestler from Waterloo, Iowa, endured one of the most disciplined workout schedules possible in preparation for the 1972 Olympics in Munich. Dan Gable trained for seven hours a day, every day for three years prior to the big event. His agony was rewarded when he won the Olympic gold medal! In fact, Dan grew accustomed to reaping rewards for his disciplined lifestyle, as he lost only one match in his entire career! (178-1)

Christians could learn much from Dan Gable's disciplined training. Often we fall far short of the disciplined maturity desired by God. God's idea is that we be trained by adversity (Hebrews 12:11). In other words, we accept trials, thank God for them, and grow stronger, deeper, and closer to Him through them! Only via this reaction will we reap the fruit of God's training.

Dan Gable did not discipline himself for the fun of it. He did it so that he might grow stronger and better prepared for Olympic competition. God disciplines us for a higher calling—to be like His Son!

QUESTIONS FOR THOUGHT AND DISCUSSION

1. Find Webster's 1828 dictionary's definition of temperance.
   What are some interesting synonyms of the word temperance?

2. The Apostle Paul uses the idea of an athlete to help us understand temperance. List some character traits that an athlete during Paul's lifetime would have exhibited.

3. Explain how the passage in Proverbs 16 can be helpful in a young person understanding more about temperance.

4. List the 7 helps to implementing Self-Control,

5. Psalm 37 gives a young person three steps in learning to commit to the Lord. What are they?

6. Give an example in the Bible of someone who sinned, but was able to repent and get back to serving God. Is there a historical example that relates?

7. Who has been given to us by Christ for help with temperance in our lives? List a few Biblical references that strengthen this argument for a believer.

ADDITIONAL HELPS
FOR THE TEMPERATE LIFE

LET THE DOGS DELIGHT TO BARK AND BITE
ISAAC WATTS

Let dogs delight to bark and bite,
For God hath made them so;
Let bears and lions growl and fight,
For 'tis their nature too.

But, children, you should never let
Such angry passions rise;
Your little hands were never made
To tear each other's eyes.

DIRTY JIM
JANE TAYLOR

Why should we bother to practice cleanliness? Aside from some
very good practical considerations, Francis Bacon reminded us
why: "For cleanness of body was ever esteemed to proceed from a
due reverence to God, to society, and to ourselves."

There was one little Jim,
'Tis reported of him,
   And must be to his lasting disgrace,

That he never was seen
With hands at all clean,
    Nor yet ever clean was his face.

His friends were much hurt,
To see so much dirt,
    And often they made him quite clean;
But all was in vain, He got dirty again,
    And not at all fit to be seen.

It gave him no pain
To hear them complain,
    Nor his own dirty clothes to survey;
His indolent mind
No pleasure could find
    In tidy and wholesome array.

The idle and bad,
Like this little land
    May love dirty ways, to be sure;
But good boys are seen,
To be decent and clean,
    Although they are ever so poor.

SELF-MASTERY
AN EXCERPT BY A. T. ROWE

It has been well said that "one does not touch real power until he has attained self-mastery; not only until he can control his passions, but until he can also dominate his environment, be greater than his surroundings."

Milton says, "He that reigns within himself, and rules his passions, his desires, and fears, is more than a king."

Herbert Spencer says, "In the supremacy of self-control consists one of the perfections of the ideal man."

The uncontrolled passion cannot be isolated, they are so far-reaching that we should by all means strive to acquire poise, self-mastery.

Passion running wild often plunges a whole family, sometimes several families, an entire community, a nation, or a world into an abyss of misery. The lack of self-mastery has strewn history with wrecks of its victims; it has ruined millions of ambitious men of rare ability and great promise.

In every quarter of the globe tragedies are being recorded every day that have been enacted when the blood was hot with anger or jealousy, and somebody did not have self-mastery. The person who has not mastered self does not carry this self-mastery into his life and is like the mariner without a compass; he is at the mercy of every wind that blows; or like the automobile without brakes or steering gear. Mrs. Oliphant says, "Prove to me that you can control yourself, and I'll say you're an educated man; but without this all other education is good for next to nothing."

"He who has mastered himself, who is his own Caesar, will be stronger than his passion, superior to circumstances, higher than his calling, greater than his speech."—Marden.

Self-mastery is not confined to being able merely to control the temper. It is much broader and more comprehensive than that. It means that when a test comes we are able to call to our aid the maximum of strength and intelligence, every atom of strength and resourcefulness, every power of mind and body with which the Creator has endowed us. When a crisis comes instead of "losing our head," becoming panic-stricken, and "flying all to pieces," we summon our resources, call upon our reserve, and go through with colors flying. The person who has not learned to control his temper or to resist his appetite, who is the victim of temptation or impulse, who is led by mere feeling or emotion and not by the steady light of principle, will never be a leader of men, for he cannot lead himself.

Nearly all the tragedies of life are caused by the lack of self-mastery. A scathing letter is written; a hot retort is made; a remark is resented. If thought had been given we should not have acted at all. Since self-mastery is so important, how shall I acquire it?

First, we are assuming that you are a Christian; if not, then you should right now, lay this book down, humble yourself before God, and ask him to forgive you and make you his child. Jesus will then become your life-pilot. This is the first step.

We must then master the secret of right-thinking. The man who has once learned to control his thought forces knows that self-mastery becomes a matter of course. He knows how to protect himself from his mental enemies as well as his physical ones.

To give no expression whatever to a passion is the surest way to kill it. If passions, great or small, are continually suppressed, they will atrophy and die from lack of expression.

HELPFUL STUDY FOR PERSONAL GROWTH

A young person who lacks temperance can expect to fall into much more serious sins as a young adult. This is revealed in Matthew 7:24-27. Years of neglect in the area of temperance can later result in a series of wrong decisions that can change a young person's whole life within a few minutes. I have personally seen this in young people, young adults and older Christians who let this area of temperance slip. God's Word clearly shows the importance of self-control. Listed below are three areas of temperance that are obviously to be put in place in a believer. You may be able to find a couple more verses and areas. Copy these verses and memorize each of them.

1. Temperance of the body: I Corinthians 9:27
2. Temperance of the thoughts: II Corinthians 10:5
3. Temperance of the emotions: Proverbs 25:28
4. _____
5. _____

PERSONAL EVALUATION
(ADAPTED FROM CHRISTIAN CHARACTER BY GARY MALDANER)

Do you have the self-control that pleases the Lord? Are you learning to be more useful to Him every day? Check those statements that describe what you are usually like.

1. Do I seem to blurt out responses in conversation when I should display temperance in my speech?

2. Am I putting practices into place daily or weekly that will help me later in life?

3. My posture is appropriate for church and school. Do I slouch? Do I appear engaged in classes or services?

4. Do I look at the person who is talking to me?

5. Am I active in fighting wrong and impure thoughts in my life?

6. Am I controlling the desire of my eyes to look at sinful things on a phone, on a computer, in books, in magazines, or on billboards? (Psalm 101:3)

7. Do I have temperance in my musical preferences?

8. Do I have temperance in my eating habits? Am I eating enough, but not overeating or constantly nibbling on candy or snack foods?

9. Am I prompt in getting out of bed in the morning?

10. Am I diligent in my studies until I have learned what I have been asked to learn?

11. Am I quick to respond in anger with my speech when someone or something irritates me?

12. When I am given a job, do I finish the job even though I may get tired and bored?

13. Do I have a habit of doing something occasionally that my body feels is unpleasant such as washing your face with cold water, eating things that you don't like without complaining, doing some physical exercise that seems too strenuous or reading something that makes me stretch mentally?

14. Do I allow things to stop me from my daily time of Bible reading and prayer?

15. Do I exhibit patience when things do not go my way? Am I patient to listen to others even when I have something to say?

QUOTES TO PONDER ON TEMPERANCE

Burton: "Conquer Thyself. Till thou hast done that thou art a slave; for it is almost as well for thee to be in subjection to another's appetite as thy own."

Milton: "He who reigns within himself, and rules passions, desires, and fears, is more than a king."

Seneca: "Most powerful is he who has himself in his power."

Hazlitt: "Those who can command themselves command others."

Walter Scott: "There never did and never will exist anything permanently noble and excellent in character which was a stranger to the exercise of resolute self-denial."

ABOUT THE AUTHOR

After serving as associate pastor for two decades, Pastor Steve Damron was voted as senior pastor of Fairhaven Baptist Church in January 2012. Growing up in Cleveland, Ohio, he attended Cleveland Baptist Church, under the leadership of Dr. Roy Thompson. Pastor Damron graduated from Fairhaven Baptist College in 1993 with a bachelor's degree in theology and continued his education earning a master's degree as well. The Damrons have been married for 23 years and have been blessed with four children—Jennifer, Sabrina, Jake, and Clint.